GORGIAS REPRINT SERIES

Volume 26

Lexical Tools
to the
Syriac New Testament

Lexical Tools to the Syriac New Testament

George Anton Kiraz

GORGIAS PRESS
2002

First Edition by Sheffield Academic Press, 1994.

Second Edition by Gorgias Press LLC, 2002

Copyright © 2002 by Gorgias Press LLC.

All rights reserved under International and Pan-American Copyright Conventions. Published in the United States of America by Gorgias Press LLC, New Jersey.

ISBN 1-931956-10-3

British Library Cataloguing in Publication Data
Kiraz, George Anton
   Lexical Tools to the Syriac New Testament
   I. Title
255.43

GORGIAS PRESS
46 Orris Ave., Piscataway, NJ 08854 USA
www.gorgiaspress.com

Printed in the United States of America

Preface

Most students of Syriac are introduced to the text of the Syriac New Testament in their first year of studies. The main task facing the student is studying the meanings of the words which constitute the text. Learning the most frequent words, moving to the less frequent ones, the student's understanding of the text expands rapidly. *Lexical Tools to the Syriac New Testament* aims to provide the student, among other aids, with such a tool.

This work is divided into ten sections, each providing the student with a different tool. Sections 1, 2 and 3 provide three frequency lists: word list, proper noun list, and a list of Syriac words derived from Greek. Section 4 consists of a list of consonantal homographs which is aimed at helping the student clarify lexical ambiguities. Each of the four sections give full morphological analysis and English meanings.

Sections 5 and 6 are devoted to the verb. The former divides the most frequent verbs into their morphological categories. The latter gives the paradigms of the most frequent verb in each category of the former section.

Sections 7 and 8 are indices: The former provides an index to all the English words which appear in this work (a more detailed English-Syriac index is given in my *Concordance to the Syriac New Testament*, vol. 6, Leiden: E. J. Brill, 1993), and the latter provides an alphabetical index of the Syriac words.

Section 9, Skeleton Syriac Grammar, is a reference grammar written by Dr Sebastian P. Brock. Finally, Section 10 provides an annotated bibliography of works which can be of use to the student.

Only frequent words which occur ten times or more in the text of the Syriac New Testament (Peshitta version) are included in this work. The text used here is based on the Syriac New Testament edition of the British and Foreign Bible Society (BFBS), now reprinted by the United Bible Society. (The original Peshitta New Testament canon does not include 2 Peter, 2 and 3 John, and Revelation; the text of these in the BFBS edition is taken from a sixth-century translation which some identify as the Philoxenian.) The lists in this work were generated from the *Syriac Electronic Data Retrieval Archive* (SEDRA), a database management system for literary and linguistic computing in Syriac.

I would like to take the opportunity to thank my *Malphono* Dr Sebastian P. Brock (Oriental Institute, University of Oxford), who suggested compiling this work, for his numerous valuable discussions, and for the use of his computer system to print this document. His Eminence Mor Clemis Augen Kaplan, Metropolitan - Patriarchal Assistant, kindly reviewed Section 6; Dr Andrew Criddle (Cambridge) and Ms Amanda Bowen (Peterhouse, Cambridge) kindly checked the cross references in Section 8 and Section 7, respectively. To Dr Philip Davies of Sheffield Academic Press, I give my gratitude for accepting this work for publication.

I have completed this book while doing research on Semitic computational morphology at the Computer Laboratory, University of Cambridge, under the direction of Dr Stephen G. Pulman (SRI International and Computer Laboratory), which was made possible by a Benefactor Studentship from St John's College.

St John's College, Cambridge
Commemoration of St. Severios the Great of Antioch,
February 11, 1993.

George Anton Kiraz

Table of Contents

Preface iii
Table of Contents iv
Abbreviations v

Section 1 1
    Word Frequency List
Section 2 35
    Proper Nouns Frequency List
Section 3 41
    Greek Frequency List
Section 4 45
    Consonantal Homographs
Section 5 51
    Verbal Forms
Section 6 57
    Verbal Paradigms
Section 7 87
    English Index
Section 8 105
    Alphabetical Syriac Index
Section 9 117
    Skeleton Syriac Grammar (by S. B. Brock)
Section 10 131
    Bibliography

Colophon

Abbreviations

act. part.	active participle
adj.	adjective
adv.	adverb
c.	common
cf.	compare
constr	construct
cont.	continue
denom.	denominative
emph.	emphatic
encl.	enclitic
f.	feminine
impf.	imperfect
impt.	imperative
inf.	infinitive
intr.	intransitive
Lat.	Latin
m.	masculine
n.	noun
num.	numeral
part.	participle
pass. part.	passive participle
perf.	perfect
pl.	plural
pr. n.	proper noun
prep.	preposition
pron.	pronoun
rad.	radical
rt.	root
s.	singular
subs.	substantive
tr.	transitive
v.	verb
w/	with
w/o	without

Section 1: Word Frequency List

Sequence.

This list is arranged according to the frequency of occurrence of words.

Format.

The list consists of four columns:

- **Column 1: Reference No.**
  Gives each word a reference number. This number is used as cross reference in other sections where the meanings of words are not given.

- **Column 2: Syriac Lexical Entry.**
  Gives the Syriac form of the word in vocalized *Serto* (Western) script.

- **Column 3: Category.**
  Gives the grammatical (i.e. morphological) category of the lexical entry.

- **Column 4: English Meanings.**
  Gives the English meanings of the lexical entry. Main English key words are given in italic. Morphological information which changes the meaning is given in bold. Greek forms of Syriac words derived from Greek are given preceding the meanings. At the right side of this column, the frequency of the lexical entry is given in italic between square brackets, [ ].

The list is divided into frequency-range groups to help the student plan study sessions. For example, the first group lists words of frequency higher than 1000.

How to Use the Frequency List.

It is important to review each group few times before going to the next one. It is quite difficult to establish associations between the Syriac words and their English meanings, since the Semitic language and the Indo-European one belong to two different families. In order to remember the meanings, therefore, it is crucial to understand the usage of the words. If the student has access to a copy of my *Concordance to the Syriac New Testament* (1993), the concordance can be consulted to learn the different forms of each word, and the usage of each form, as they appear in the New Testament.

Word Frequency List: 1 - 28

Ref.	Syriac	Cat.	Meaning	

Words occurring 1085 - 4234 times:

Ref.	Syriac	Cat.	Meaning	
1	ܠ	particle	for, to	[4234]
2	ܠܐ	particle	no, not	[3140]
3	ܗܘܐ	v.	be, (as enclitic) was, turn out	[3041]
4	ܡܢ	particle	from	[2966]
5	ܐܡܪ	v.	say, speak	[2551]
6	ܕܝܢ	particle	but, yet	[1828]
7	ܗܘ	pron.	he, (as enclitic) is, it	[1792]
8	ܐܢܐ	pron.	I	[1728]
9	ܗܢܐ	pron.	this	[1578]
10	ܥܠ	particle	about, concerning, on	[1549]
11	ܐܢܬ	pron.	thou	[1401]
12	ܟܠ + ܟܘܠ	particle	all, entirely, every, whole	[1400]
13	ܐܠܗܐ	n. m.	a god, God	[1389]
14	ܗܘ	pron.	that, those, w/ ܕ he who	[1256]
15	ܟܕ	particle	when, while, after	[1214]
16	ܐܝܬ	subs.	are, is	[1100]
17	ܓܝܪ	particle	Gr. γάρ for	[1085]

Words occurring 602 - 966 times:

Ref.	Syriac	Cat.	Meaning	
18	ܐܬܐ	v.	come; Afᶜel bring	[966]
19	ܐܝܢܐ	pron.	what, which, who	[858]
20	ܒ	particle	in, among, with, by, at	[824]
21	ܐܠܐ	particle	but, but rather	[799]
22	ܒܪܐ	n. m.	son	[786]
23	ܐܦ	particle	also, even	[765]
24	ܐܝܟ	particle	according to, as	[759]
25	ܡܪܝܐ	n. m.	lord, master	[755]
26	ܡܛܠ	particle	because	[740]
27	ܚܕ	num.	ܚܕ ܚܕ each one, one, (as adj) certain one	[739]
28	ܚܙܐ	v.	see, behold	[734]

Ref.	Syriac	Cat.	Meaning	
29	ܥܡ	particle	with	[723]
30	ܐܢܫܐ	n. c.	person, mankind, people	[709]
31	ܥܒܕ	v.	make, do, perform, act, celebrate (a feast); Šaf ͨ el subdue, subject	[706]
32	ܝܕܥ	v.	know; Af ͨ el make known; Eštaf ͨ al recognize	[704]
33	ܐܢ	particle	if	[680]
34	ܠܘܬ	particle	toward, to, against	[602]

Words occurring 405 - 586 times:

35	ܡܫܝܚܐ	pp.	Anointed One, Christ, Messiah	[586]
36	ܩܡ	v.	rise, stand; Pa ͨͨ el establish; Af ͨ el cause to stand	[550]
37	ܝܗܒ	v.	give	[534]
38	ܫܡܥ	v.	hear, obey; Af ͨ el cause to hear	[494]
39	ܡܕܡ	n. c.	something	[492]
40	ܪܘܚܐ	n. c.	breath, spirit, wind	[478]
41	ܐܒܐ	n. m.	father	[453]
42	ܐܫܟܚ	v.	be able, find, happen	[448]
43	ܐܙܠ	v.	depart, go	[447]
44	ܣܓܝܐܐ	adj.	many, much	[439]
45	ܒܝܬܐ	n. m.	abode, house	[431]
46	ܢܦܫܐ	n. f.	soul, self, breath of life	[422]
47	ܥܠܡܐ	n. m.	age, eternity, world	[413]
48	ܡܠܬܐ	n. f.	word	[409]
49	ܢܦܩ	v.	go out, w/ ܪܘܚܐ defend; Ethpa ͨͨ al be exercised; Af ͨ el make cast out	[405]

Words occurring 305 - 395 times:

50	ܪܒܐ	adj.	chief, great, w/ suffix master	[395]
51	ܝܘܡܐ	n. m.	day	[380]
52	ܡܢ	pron.	w/ ܕ he who, who	[367]
53	ܐܝܕܐ	n. f.	hand, w/ ܥܠ near, w/ ܒ through	[362]

Ref.	Syriac	Cat.	Meaning	
54	ܐܚܐ	n. m.	brother	[360]
55	ܡܠܠ	v.	Pa``el`` speak	[350]
56	ܩܪܐ	v.	call, read, w/ ܥܠ appeal to	[330]
57	ܥܡܐ	n. m.	nation, people; pl. Gentiles	[324]
58	ܓܒܪܐ	n. m.	husband, man	[319]
59	ܒܥܐ	v.	seek for, inquire into, question, require	[313]
60	ܫܡܝܐ	n. c.	heaven, sky	[309]
61	ܐܝܟܢܐ	particle	as, how	[308]
62	ܗܝܡܢ	v.	believe, trust in	[305]

Words occurring 250 - 296 times:

Ref.	Syriac	Cat.	Meaning	
63	ܐܘ	particle	else, or, rather than	[296]
64	ܐܚܪܢܐ	adj.	another	[295]
65	ܩܕܡ	particle	before	[290]
66	ܡܢܐ	pron.	what, why	[289]
67	ܗܟܢܐ	particle	thus	[282]
68	ܬܠܡܝܕܐ	n. m.	disciple	[277]
69	ܨܒܐ	v.	desire, will	[273]
70	ܐܪܥܐ	n. f.	country, earth, ground, land, soil	[272]
71	ܗܐ	particle	behold!, lo!	[270]
72	ܗܝܡܢܘܬܐ	n. f.	belief, faith	[264]
73	ܥܠ	v.	enter; Af``el`` bring in	[264]
74	ܒܬܪ	particle	after, behind	[256]
75	ܗܟܝܠ	particle	hence, therefore	[250]

Words occurring 200 - 249 times:

Ref.	Syriac	Cat.	Meaning	
76	ܫܪܐ	v.	loosen, lodge; Pa``el`` begin; Ethpa``el`` eat a meal, be loosened	[249]
77	ܩܪܒ	v.	come, draw near, touch; Pa``el`` bring near, bring near, offer; Af``el`` fight	[244]
78	ܫܡܐ	n. m.	name	[244]

Ref.	Syriac	Cat.	Meaning	
79	ܡܫܐܠ	v.	ask, inquire, w/ ܫܠܡܐ salute; Af^{c}el lend	[243]
80	ܐܢܬܬܐ	n. f.	wife, woman	[238]
81	ܡܐ	pron.	what	[236]
82	ܫܕܪ	v.	Pa^{cc}el send	[235]
83	ܒܪܢܫܐ	n. c.	= ܒܪ + ܐܢܫܐ human, person	[231]
84	ܟܬܒ	v.	write	[231]
85	ܢܣܒ	v.	take, receive, w/ ܐܦܐ be a hypocrite	[229]
86	ܙܒܢܐ	n. m.	time, season, period	[227]
87	ܢܡܘܣܐ	n. m.	Gr. νόμος law	[224]
88	ܕܝܠ	particle	own	[223]
89	ܠܝܬ	subs.	is not	[223]
90	ܡܕܝܢܬܐ	n. f.	city, town	[223]
91	ܥܕܡܐ	particle	until	[219]
92	ܫܒܩ	v.	allow, forgive, leave	[217]
93	ܛܒܐ	adj.	good, ܛܒ as adv. much	[214]
94	ܣܡ	v.	place, put	[207]
95	ܬܡܢ	particle	there	[206]
96	ܝܗܘܕܝܐ	adj.	Jew	[205]
97	ܬܪܝܢ	num.	two	[204]
98	ܩܒܠ	v.	accuse, appeal to; Pa^{cc}el receive, take; Saf^{c}el oppose, be present	[200]
99	ܫܠܡ	v.	be completed; Ethp^{c}el be delivered up; Pa^{cc}el complete; Af^{c}el deliver up	[200]

Words occurring 150 - 193 times:

100	ܗܫܐ	particle	now	[193]
101	ܬܘܒ	particle	again, furthermore	[192]
102	ܥܒܕܐ	n. m.	deed, work	[191]
103	ܒܝܫܐ	adj.	evil, wrong	[185]
104	ܡܠܐܟܐ	n. m.	angel, messenger	[181]
105	ܪܫܐ	n. m.	head, beginning; pl. chiefs	[181]
106	ܐܟܠ	v.	eat, consume, w/ ܩܪܨ accuse; Af^{c}el feed	[178]

Ref.	Syriac	Cat.	Meaning	
107	ܟܢܫܐ	n. m.	assembly, crowd, gathering (of persons), multitude	[178]
108	ܚܝܐ	n. m.	life, salvation	[177]
109	ܦܓܪܐ	n. m.	body	[176]
110	ܡܝܬ	v.	die, be dead; Af˘el put to death	[171]
111	ܗܝܕܝܢ	particle	afterwards, next, then	[169]
112	ܐܚܕ	v.	hold, take, apprehend, maintain, close (a door); Af˘el w/ ܢܘܪܐ kindle, let out	[168]
113	ܠܒܐ	n. m.	heart	[168]
114	ܡܠܟܘܬܐ	n. f.	kingdom, realm, reign	[167]
115	ܢܒܝܐ	n. m.	prophet; f. prophetess	[167]
116	ܡܠܐ	v.	complete, fill	[166]
117	ܚܝܐ	v.	live; Af˘el make live, save	[165]
118	ܫܠܡܐ	n. m.	peace, salutation, w/ ܝܗܒ salute	[164]
119	ܫܩܠ	v.	bear, take up	[160]
120	ܥܢܐ	v.	answer	[158]
121	ܢܦܠ	v.	fall	[157]
122	ܥܝܢܐ	n. f.	eye	[155]
123	ܛܝܒܘܬܐ	n. f.	grace, favour, goodness, graciousess, kindness	[154]
124	ܩܠܐ	n. m.	voice	[153]
125	ܚܝܠܐ	n. m.	power, strength, virtue, force, mighty work	[150]

Words occurring 125 - 148 times:

Ref.	Syriac	Cat.	Meaning	
126	ܝܬܒ	v.	sit; Af˘el establish, seat	[148]
127	ܩܕܝܫܐ	adj.	holy, saint	[148]
128	ܐܡܝܢ	particle	verily, Amen	[147]
129	ܝܠܦ	v.	learn; Pa˘˘el teach	[147]
130	ܐܦܐ	n. f.	face, w/ ܢܣܒ hypocrite, w/ ܠܚܡ presence-bread	[143]
131	ܫܥܬܐ	n. f.	hour	[142]
132	ܥܒܕܐ	n. m.	servant	[141]
133	ܪܡܐ	v.	cast, place, put	[136]
134	ܣܠܩ	v.	ascend, go up; Af˘el make ascend	[134]

Ref.	Syriac	Cat.	Meaning	
135	ܡܠܟܐ	n. m.	king; f. queen	[130]
136	ܢܛܪ	v.	guard, keep, observe, reserve	[130]
137	ܦܩܕ	v.	command	[130]
138	ܒܣܪܐ	n. m.	flesh	[129]
139	ܒܠܚܘܕ	adv.	alone, only	[128]
140	ܡܝܬܐ	pp.	dead	[126]
141	ܡܢܘ	pron.	= ܡܢ + ܗܘ who is this?	[126]
142	ܬܠܬܐ	num.	three	[126]
143	ܚܘܒܐ	n. m.	love, lovingkindness	[125]
144	ܡܘܬܐ	n. m.	death	[125]

Words occurring 110 - 124 times:

Ref.	Syriac	Cat.	Meaning	
145	ܩܛܠ	v.	kill	[124]
146	ܟܗܢܐ	n. m.	priest	[121]
147	ܝܠܕ	v.	bear (a child); Af`el beget	[120]
148	ܛܝܒ	v.	Pa``el prepare	[120]
149	ܪܚܡ	v.	love, have mercy; Pa``el have compassion; Ethpa``al have mercy	[119]
150	ܕܢ	denom.	judge	[118]
151	ܣܗܕ	v.	testify, witness	[118]
152	ܗܝܟܠܐ	n. m.	sanctuary, temple	[117]
153	ܚܠܦ	particle	for, instead	[117]
154	ܐܬܪܐ	n. m.	country, place, region, respite, available space or room	[116]
155	ܕܚܠ	v.	fear; Pa``el cause to fear	[114]
156	ܣܒܪ	denom.	Pa``el declare, preach; Pai`el bear, endure; Ethpai`al be fed	[113]
157	ܥܕܬܐ	n. f.	assembly, church, congregation	[113]
158	ܗܠܟ	v.	Pa``el walk	[110]

Ref.	Syriac	Cat.	Meaning	

Words occurring 100 - 109 times:

Ref.	Syriac	Cat.	Meaning	
159	ܐܝܟܐ	particle	where	[109]
160	ܝܡܐ	n. m.	sea	[108]
161	ܢܚܬ	v.	descend	[108]
162	ܣܒܪ	v.	consider, suppose, think; Pa^{cc}el hope	[108]
163	ܥܒܪ	v.	cross over, w/ ܥܠ transgress, w/ ܡܢ turn away from; Af^cel pass over	[108]
164	ܫܦܝܪܐ	adj.	beautiful, good, well	[108]
165	ܐܘܪܚܐ	n. f.	road, way, highway, journeying	[105]
166	ܟܢܫ	v.	assemble, gather	[105]
167	ܚܒ	v.	be kindled; Pa^{cc}el love	[103]
168	ܣܟܠܐ	n. m.	sin	[103]
169	ܩܕܡܝܐ	adj.	first, fore	[103]
170	ܟܬܒܐ	n. m.	book, writing, Scripture	[102]
171	ܦܪܝܫܐ	pp.	Pharisee	[102]
172	ܕܝܢܐ	n. m.	judgement, sentence (of judge)	[101]
173	ܪܚܢܐ	n. m.	desire, will	[101]
174	ܝܬܝܪܐ	adj.	better, excelling, excessive, greater, more	[100]
175	ܨܠܝ	v.	incline toward, heed; Pa^{cc}el pray	[100]
176	ܪܓܠܐ	n. f.	foot	[100]
177	ܫܒܥܐ	num.	seven	[100]

Words occurring 91 - 99 times:

Ref.	Syriac	Cat.	Meaning	
178	ܩܘܕܫܐ	n. m.	holiness, sanctuary	[99]
179	ܐܬܫܒܘܚܬܐ	n. f.	glory, praise	[99]
180	ܓܠܐ	v.	manifest, reveal	[98]
181	ܠܚܡܐ	n. m.	bread, w/ ܐܦܐ shewbread	[98]
182	ܚܘܐ	v.	Pa^{cc}el show	[97]
183	ܩܘܐ	denom.	Pa^{cc}el abide, remain	[97]
184	ܕܡܐ	n. m.	blood	[96]
185	ܟܠܢܫ	n. c.	= ܟܠ + ܐܢܫ every one	[96]

Ref.	Syriac	Cat.	Meaning	
186	ܫܒܚ	denom.	Pa``cc``el commend, glorify, praise	[95]
187	ܟܪܙ	denom.	Ethp``c``el be preached, be proclaimed; Af``c``el preach	[94]
188	ܡܝ̈ܐ	n. m.	water	[94]
189	ܫܪܪܐ	n. m.	truth	[94]
190	ܐܡܐ	n. f.	mother	[93]
191	ܕܒܪ	v.	conduct, lead, take	[93]
192	ܦܘܩܕܢܐ	n. m.	commandment, decree, edict, precept	[92]
193	ܗܦܟ	v.	return, turn; Ethpa``cc``al conduct oneself	[91]

Words occurring 86 - 89 times:

194	ܚܝܐ	adj.	alive, living	[89]
195	ܫܘܒܚܐ	n. m.	glorification, glory, praise	[89]
196	ܐܒܕ	v.	perish; Af``c``el destroy, lose	[87]
197	ܕܠܡܐ	particle	lest	[87]
198	ܚܛܝܬܐ	n. f.	sin	[87]
199	ܐܦܠܐ	particle	= ܐܦ + ܠܐ not even	[86]
200	ܦܘܡܐ	n. m.	mouth, edge	[86]
201	ܫܘܐ	v.	be equal, worthy; Ethp``c``el agree; Pa``cc``el spread, wipe; Af``c``el smooth	[86]
202	ܫܠܝܚܐ	pp.	apostle, sent one	[86]

Words occurring 80 - 84 times:

203	ܕܚܠܬܐ	n. f.	awe, fear	[84]
204	ܦܬܚ	v.	open	[84]
205	ܩܫܝܫܐ	n. m.	elder	[84]
206	ܟܠܡܕܡ	idiom	everything	[83]
207	ܐܬܐ	n. f.	miraculous token, sign	[82]
208	ܝܕܐ	v.	Af``c``el confess, give thanks; Eštaf``c``al profess, promise	[82]
209	ܠܒܪ	particle	outside	[82]
210	ܢܘܪܐ	n. f.	fire	[81]
211	ܦܐܪܐ	n. m.	fruit	[81]

Ref.	Syriac	Cat.	Meaning	
212	ܩܪܐ	v.	w/ ܒ appeal to, cry aloud	[81]
213	ܐܫܬܝ	v.	drink	[81]
214	ܛܠܝܐ	n. m.	boy, youth; f. girl, maid	[80]
215	ܥܡܕ	v.	sink, be baptized; Af‑el baptize	[80]
216	ܫܘܠܛܢܐ	n. m.	authority, dominion, power	[80]

Words occurring 75 - 79 times:

Ref.	Syriac	Cat.	Meaning	
217	ܝܬܪ	v.	gain, remain over, w/ ܡܢ prefer; Pa‑‑el make abound; Af‑el benefit	[79]
218	ܝܬܝܪܐܝܬ	adv.	abundantly, especially, exceedingly	[78]
219	ܪܥܝܢܐ	n. m.	mind, idea, thought, conception, w/ ܣܟܠ fool	[77]
220	ܬܪܥܐ	n. m.	door, gate	[77]
221	ܚܕܝ	v.	rejoice, be glad; Pa‑‑el gladden	[76]
222	ܛܥܐ	v.	wander, go astray, err, forget; Af‑el lead astray, deceive, delude	[76]
223	ܟܢܘܫܬܐ	n. f.	council, synagogue	[76]
224	ܣܦܪܐ	n. m.	lawyer, scribe	[76]
225	ܘܠܐ	adj.	part. it proper, it is right	[75]
226	ܬܪܥܣܪ	num.	twelve	[75]

Words occurring 70 - 74 times:

Ref.	Syriac	Cat.	Meaning	
227	ܐܣܐ	v.	Pa‑‑el heal	[74]
228	ܫܪܒܬܐ	n. f.	family, generation, line, stock, tribe	[74]
229	ܟܡܐ	particle	how many?, how much?	[73]
230	ܬܚܝܬ	particle	under	[73]
231	ܙܒܢ	v.	buy; Pa‑‑el sell	[72]
232	ܫܢܬܐ	n. f.	year	[72]
233	ܕܡܐ	v.	resemble; Pa‑‑el compare, liken to	[70]
234	ܛܝܒ	v.	Pa‑‑el make ready	[70]

Ref.	Syriac	Cat.	Meaning	
__	__	__	__	__

Words occurring 66 - 69 times:

Ref.	Syriac	Cat.	Meaning	
235	ܐܬܪܐ	n. f.	place	[69]
236	ܟܐܦܐ	n. f.	rock, stone	[69]
237	ܩܠܝܠܐ	adj.	light, little, swift	[69]
238	ܫܒܬܐ	n. f.	Sabbath	[69]
239	ܕܟܐ	v.	Paᶜᶜel cleanse	[68]
240	ܗܢܘ	pron.	= ܗܢܐ + ܗܘ this is he	[68]
241	ܠܠܝܐ	n. m.	night	[68]
242	ܢܘܗܪܐ	n. m.	light	[68]
243	ܚܝܘܬܐ	n. f.	animal, living creature	[67]
244	ܟܐܢܘܬܐ	n. f.	uprightness, rectitude, righteousness, justice	[67]
245	ܣܗܕܘܬܐ	n. f.	testimony	[67]
246	ܩܪܝܬܐ	n. f.	field, village	[67]
247	ܙܥܘܪܐ	adj.	little, least	[66]
248	ܚܫܒ	v.	think, reckon, deliberate	[66]
249	ܛܘܪܐ	n. m.	hill, mountain	[66]
250	ܝܘܠܦܢܐ	n. m.	teaching, instruction, doctrine	[66]
251	ܡܛܐ	v.	arrive, reach; Paᶜᶜel attain	[66]
252	ܦܝܣ	denom.	Gr. πεῖσαι Afᶜel convince, persuade	[66]
253	ܦܠܚ	v.	work, cultivate, labour; Afᶜel make serve	[66]

Words occurring 60 - 65 times:

Ref.	Syriac	Cat.	Meaning	
254	ܐܣܪ	v.	bind, fasten	[65]
255	ܚܒܝܒܐ	adj.	beloved	[65]
256	ܠܘܩܒܠ	particle	against, near, opposite to, w/ ܩܡ resist	[65]
257	ܥܬܝܕܐ	adj.	steadfast, true	[65]
258	ܕܡܘܬܐ	n. f.	exemplar, form, image, pattern, similitude, type	[64]
259	ܚܕܘܬܐ	n. f.	gladness, joy	[64]
260	ܪܕܐ	v.	flow, journey, instruct, chastise	[63]
261	ܚܪ	v.	look, behold	[62]
262	ܠܡܐ	pron.	why	[61]

Ref.	Syriac	Cat.	Meaning	
263	ܡܚܕܐ	particle	at once, immediately	[61]
264	ܣܓܕ	v.	worship, pay homage	[61]
265	ܫܡܫ	v.	Pa``el minister, serve	[60]

Words occurring 55 - 59 times:

266	ܐܘܠܨܢܐ	n. m.	affliction, oppression, tribulation	[59]
267	ܐܪܒܥܐ	num.	four	[59]
268	ܚܕܬܐ	adj.	new	[59]
269	ܟܘܪܣܝܐ	n. m.	seat, throne	[59]
270	ܣܒܪܐ	n. m.	hope	[59]
271	ܒܪܟ	v.	kneel; Pa``el bless	[58]
272	ܙܕܩ	v.	P`al part. fitting, it is right; Pa``el approve, justify	[58]
273	ܠܫܢܐ	n. m.	tongue, language	[58]
274	ܪܡ	v.	be high; Af`el exalt	[58]
275	ܐܠܘ	particle	if	[57]
276	ܐܡܬܝ	particle	when?	[57]
277	ܐܣܝܪܐ	pp.	bound, prisoner	[57]
278	ܥܡܪ	v.	dwell	[57]
279	ܦܢܐ	v.	return; Pa``el answer, give back; Af`el cause to turn	[57]
280	ܦܪܫ	v.	separate, appoint	[57]
281	ܒܛܠ	v.	be idle; Pa``el annul	[56]
282	ܠܘܩܕܡ	particle	before, formerly	[56]
283	ܡܐܢܐ	n. m.	garment, receptacle, utensil, vessel	[56]
284	ܡܟܝܠ	particle	henceforth, now, therefore	[56]
285	ܣܥܪ	v.	do, effect, visit	[55]

Words occurring 50 - 54 times:

286	ܦܪܩ	v.	deliver, save, depart; Pa``el pursue, rescue; Af`el go away, abstain from	[54]
287	ܩܪܝܒܐ	adj.	at hand, near, neighbour	[54]
288	ܐܚܪܝܐ	adj.	last, extreme	[53]

Ref.	Syriac	Cat.	Meaning	
289	ܚܟܡܬܐ	n. f.	wisdom	[53]
290	ܫܠܝܛܐ	adj.	lawful, permitted, (pl) magistrates, (pl) rulers	[53]
291	ܘܗܪ	v.	Ethpa''al marvel, be amazed	[52]
292	ܚܫܘܟܐ	adj.	dark, darkness (dark place)	[52]
293	ܝܡܝܢܐ	n. f.	right	[52]
294	ܟܠܝܘܡ	idiom	always	[52]
295	ܠܡܢܐ	pron.	why	[52]
296	ܩܕܡ	v.	go before	[52]
297	ܬܫܡܫܬܐ	n. f.	ministration, service, attendance	[52]
298	ܗܘܪܟܐ	particle	hence, here	[51]
299	ܙܩܦ	v.	crucify, elevate, erect, lift up	[50]
300	ܙܪܥ	v.	sow	[50]
301	ܙܪܥܐ	n. m.	seed	[50]
302	ܠܒܫ	v.	put on, be clothed; Af''el clothe	[50]

Words occurring 48 and 49 times:

Ref.	Syriac	Cat.	Meaning	
303	ܒܝܬ	particle	between	[49]
304	ܚܛܝܐ	adj.	sinner	[49]
305	ܚܡܫܐ	num.	five	[49]
306	ܝܕܥܬܐ	n. f.	knowledge	[49]
307	ܣܛܢܐ	n. m.	adversary, as prop. n. Satan	[49]
308	ܣܟܠ	v.	Pa''el make understand; Ethpa''al understand	[49]
309	ܨܠܘܬܐ	n. f.	prayer	[49]
310	ܐܠܦܐ	num.	thousand	[48]
311	ܘܝ	particle	alas for!, woe!	[48]
312	ܚܒ	v.	owe, be condemned; Pa''el condemn	[48]
313	ܣܒܪܬܐ	n. f.	message, good tidings, Gospel	[48]
314	ܫܐܕܐ	n. m.	demon, evil spirit	[48]

Words occurring 45 - 47 times:

Ref.	Syriac	Cat.	Meaning	
315	ܒܢܐ	v.	build	[47]

Ref.	Syriac	Cat.	Meaning	
316	ܙܕܝܩܐ	adj.	*just, righteous*	[47]
317	ܦܠܓ	v.	*distribute, divide*; Ethpᶜel *divide, doubt*	[47]
318	ܒܝܬ	particle	*between*	[46]
319	ܡܗܝܡܢܐ	n. m.	*believer, believing*	[46]
320	ܡܘܗܒܬܐ	n. f.	*gift*	[46]
321	ܡܬܠܐ	n. m.	*parable, proverb, similitude*	[46]
322	ܣܡܟ	v.	*recline* to eat, *support*; Afᶜel *cause to recline*	[46]
323	ܪܗܛ	v.	*run*	[46]
324	ܐܕܢܐ	n. f.	*ear*	[45]
325	ܐܠܦܐ	n. f.	*boat, ship*	[45]
326	ܫܒܚ	denom.	Šafᶜel *glorify*; Eštafᶜal *pride* oneself	[45]
327	ܚܝܒܐ	adj.	*debtor*	[45]
328	ܚܣܢ	v.	*gird, strike*	[45]
329	ܡܝܩܕܡܬ	pp.	*before*, w/ ܡܢ *before*, w/ ܡܢ *formerly*	[45]

Words occurring 43 and 44 times:

330	ܒܥܠܐ	n. m.	*husband, lord, master*	[44]
331	ܓܒܐ	v.	*choose, elect, collect* (tribute or tax); Paᶜᶜel *gather*	[44]
332	ܗܘܝܘ	pron.	= ܗܘ + ܗܘ i.e., *that is to say*	[44]
333	ܙܥ	v.	*stir, be shaken, be confused*; Afᶜel *trouble, stir* up	[44]
334	ܟܦܪ	v.	*deny, refuse*	[44]
335	ܡܠܦܢܐ	n. m.	*teacher*	[44]
336	ܪܥܐ	denom.	Ethpaᶜᶜal *think*	[43]

Words occurring 40 - 42 times:

337	ܛܘܒܐ	n. m.	*beatitude, blessedness, happiness*	[42]
338	ܝܘܡܢܐ	n. m.	*to-day*	[42]
339	ܡܠܟ	v.	*counsel, promise*; Ethpaᶜᶜal *deliberate*; Afᶜel *reign*	[42]
340	ܥܪܩ	v.	*flee*	[42]
341	ܐܠܨ	v.	*constrain, urge*	[41]
342	ܒܟܐ	v.	*weep*	[41]

Ref.	Syriac	Cat.	Meaning	
343	ܒܪܬܐ	n. f.	daughter, constr. w/ ܩܠܐ utterance, word	[41]
344	ܙܗܪ	v.	Ethpᶜel w/ ܡܢ beware of, w/ ܒ take care of, take heed; Paᶜᶜel warn	[41]
345	ܣܘܦܐ	n. f.	end	[41]
346	ܝܩܪ	v.	be heavy, be precious; Paᶜᶜel honour; Afᶜel make heavy	[41]
347	ܡܫܡܫܢܐ	n. m.	attendant, minister, servant	[41]
348	ܢܩܦ	v.	adhere, cleave to, follow	[41]
349	ܣܡܝܐ	adj.	blind	[41]
350	ܣܢܐ	v.	hate	[41]
351	ܓܡܪ	v.	accomplish, fulfil, mature, perfect	[40]
352	ܕܗܒܐ	n. m.	gold	[40]
353	ܙܕܝܩܘܬܐ	n. f.	justness, righteousness, uprightness	[40]
354	ܢܚ	v.	cease, rest; Afᶜel put off, refresh, give rest	[40]
355	ܢܣܐ	v.	Paᶜᶜel prove, tempt, try	[40]
356	ܥܝܪ	v.	Afᶜel arouse, wake up; Ettafᶜal watch, be awake	[40]
357	ܫܪܟܐ	n. m.	remainder, residue, rest	[40]

Words occurring 38 and 39 times:

Ref.	Syriac	Cat.	Meaning	
358	ܐܝܩܪܐ	n. m.	honour, glory, majesty	[39]
359	ܐܡܪܐ	n. m.	lamb, young sheep	[39]
360	ܚܛܐ	v.	err, sin	[39]
361	ܟܣܦܐ	n. m.	money, silver	[39]
362	ܟܪܟ	v.	wrap; Ethpᶜel go around; Afᶜel lead about	[39]
363	ܣܦܝܢܬܐ	n. f.	boat, ship, sailing vessel	[39]
364	ܥܘܠܐ	n. m.	iniquity, unrighteousness	[39]
365	ܪܚܡܐ	n. m.	bowels, mercy	[39]
366	ܪܡܐ	adj.	high, w/ ܩܠܐ loud voice	[39]
367	ܒܥܠܕܒܒܐ	adj.	enemy	[38]
368	ܕܓܠܐ	adj.	false, liar	[38]
369	ܗܕܡܐ	n. m.	limb, member	[38]
370	ܡܘܠܟܢܐ	n. m.	promise	[38]

Ref.	Syriac	Cat.	Meaning	
371	ܡܣܟܢܐ	adj.	poor	[38]
372	ܪܘܓܙܐ	n. m.	anger, indignation, wrath	[38]
373	ܫܕܐ	v.	cast, throw	[38]
374	ܬܒ	v.	repent, return; Af‍ʿel answer, vomit	[38]

Words occurring 35 - 37 times:

375	ܒܗܬ	v.	be ashamed; Af‍ʿel shame	[37]
376	ܚܡܪܐ	n. m.	wine	[37]
377	ܚܟܝܡܐ	adj.	wise, prudent, cunning (words)	[36]
378	ܦܪܥ	v.	recompense	[36]
379	ܩܝܡܬܐ	n. f.	resurrection	[36]
380	ܫܪܝܪܐܝܬ	adv.	truly	[36]
381	ܚܒܠ	v.	Pa‍ʿʿel destroy, corrupt, alter	[35]
382	ܚܫ	v.	suffer, feel	[35]
383	ܕܟܪ	v.	remember; Af‍ʿel cause to remember	[35]
384	ܥܬܝܪܐ	adj.	rich, wealthy	[35]
385	ܦܪܨܘܦܐ	n. m.	Gr. πρόσωπον aspect, countenance, face, person	[35]
386	ܪܒܐ	v.	grow up, increase; Pa‍ʿʿel cause increase, nourish	[35]
387	ܫܢܐ	v.	be mad; Pa‍ʿʿel depart, remove	[35]
388	ܫܪ	v.	be strong; Pa‍ʿʿel establish; Af‍ʿel believe, strengthen	[35]

Words occurring 33 and 34 times:

389	ܐܝܢ	particle	yea, so, truly	[34]
390	ܓܕܦ	v.	Pa‍ʿʿel blaspheme	[34]
391	ܕܡܟ	v.	sleep	[34]
392	ܝܡܐ	v.	take an oath, swear; Af‍ʿel make swear	[34]
393	ܠܘ	pron.	= ܠܐ + ܗܘ no, not	[34]
394	ܦܣܩ	v.	cut down, cut off; Pa‍ʿʿel break	[34]
395	ܪܕܦ	v.	follow, persecute	[34]
396	ܓܙܘܪܬܐ	n. f.	circumcision	[33]
397	ܕܟܪ	v.	Ethp‍ʿel remember; Af‍ʿel remind, make mention of	[33]

Ref.	Syriac	Cat.	Meaning	
398	ܟܣܐ	n. m.	*cup*	[*33*]
399	ܥܠܬܐ	n. f.	*cause, occasion*	[*33*]
400	ܨܒܘܬܐ	n. f.	*affair, matter, thing*	[*33*]
401	ܫܡܫܐ	n. c.	*sun*	[*33*]

Words occurring 31 and 32 times:

402	ܐܦܢ	particle	*even if*	[*32*]
403	ܒܪܡ	particle	*but, nevertheless, yet*	[*32*]
404	ܒܥܓܠ	particle	*quickly*	[*32*]
405	ܩܒܪܐ	n. m.	*sepulchre, tomb*	[*32*]
406	ܐܓܪܐ	n. m.	*pay, recompense, reward*	[*31*]
407	ܕܝܘܐ	n. m.	*demon, devil*	[*31*]
408	ܕܝܬܩܐ	n. f.	Gr. διαθήκη *covenant, testament*	[*31*]
409	ܙܟܐ	v.	*overcome*	[*31*]
410	ܛܡܐ	adj.	*defiled, filthy, impure, unclean*	[*31*]
411	ܟܣܐ	v.	*conceal, cover, hide*	[*31*]
412	ܡܣܝܒܪܢܘܬܐ	n. f.	*endurance, patience*	[*31*]
413	ܡܥܡܘܕܝܬܐ	n. f.	*baptism, washing*	[*31*]
414	ܩܘܪܒܢܐ	n. m.	*gift, offering*	[*31*]
415	ܩܘܫܬܐ	n. m.	*truth, verity*	[*31*]
416	ܫܦܪ	v.	*please*	[*31*]

Words occurring 30 times:

417	ܐܘܢܓܠܝܘܢ	n. m.	Gr. εὐαγγέλιον *Gospel*	[*30*]
418	ܐܝܡܡܐ	n. m.	*daytime*	[*30*]
419	ܓܘ	particle	*in, within*	[*30*]
420	ܚܘܪܒܐ	n. m.	*desolation, wilderness*	[*30*]
421	ܝܨܦ	v.	*be anxious, be careful, be solicitous*	[*30*]
422	ܝܩܕ	v.	*burn;* Af^{c}el *set* (on fire)	[*30*]
423	ܟܪܗ	v.	*be sick, be weak*	[*30*]
424	ܬܩܠ	v.	Ethp^{c}el *be offended;* Af^{c}el *make stumble*	[*30*]

Ref.	Syriac	Cat.	Meaning	
425	ܣܓܝ	v.	increase, be great; Af`el multiply	[30]
426	ܣܗܕܐ	n. m.	martyr, witness	[30]
427	ܥܕܟܝܠ	particle	still, yet	[30]
428	ܫܥܐ	v.	Ethp`el play; Ethpa``al narrate	[30]

Words occurring 28 and 29 times:

Ref.	Syriac	Cat.	Meaning	
429	ܚܒܪܐ	n. m.	associate, companion, comrade, friend, neighbour	[29]
430	ܟܐܐ	v.	rebuke, reprove	[29]
431	ܟܪܝܗܐ	pp.	infirm, sick, weak (in faith)	[29]
432	ܡܨܥܬܐ	n. f.	middle, midst	[29]
433	ܢܒܐ	v.	Ethpa``al prophesy	[29]
434	ܢܓܕ	v.	drag, draw, lead, withdraw; Pa``el beat, scourge; Ethpa``al be beaten	[29]
435	ܢܗܪ	v.	shine; Pa``el explain, bring to light; Af`el illumine	[29]
436	ܢܘܢܐ	n. m.	fish	[29]
437	ܥܕ	particle	until, while	[29]
438	ܪܚܡܐ	n. m.	friend	[29]
439	ܐܓܪܬܐ	n. f.	epistle, letter	[28]
440	ܐܪܙܐ	n. m.	mystery	[28]
441	ܒܣܡ	v.	Pa``el comfort, encourage	[28]
442	ܚܙܘܐ	n. m.	appearance, aspect, apparition	[28]
443	ܟܘܟܒܐ	n. m.	star, planet	[28]
444	ܟܘܡܪܐ	n. m.	priest	[28]
445	ܟܪܐ	v.	sorrow; Pa``el shorten; Af`el make sorry	[28]
446	ܠܥܣ	v.	eat	[28]
447	ܡܐܟܘܠܬܐ	n. f.	food	[28]
448	ܣܟܐ	v.	Pa``el expect, look for	[28]
449	ܥܢܢܐ	n. f.	cloud	[28]
450	ܥܪܣܐ	n. f.	bed, bier, pallet	[28]
451	ܦܨܚܐ	n. m.	Feast of Passover	[28]
452	ܪܫܝܬܐ	n. f.	beginning, (pl) first fruits	[28]

Ref.	Syriac	Cat.	Meaning	

Words occurring 26 and 27 times:

Ref.	Syriac	Cat.	Meaning	
453	ܐܪܡܠܬܐ	n. f.	widow	[27]
454	ܓܠܝܢܐ	n. m.	assurance, revelation, the Apocalypse	[27]
455	ܕܝܢܐ	n. m.	judge	[27]
456	ܟܪܣܐ	n. f.	belly, womb	[27]
457	ܠܒܘܫܐ	n. m.	garment	[27]
458	ܡܥܒܪܐ	n. m.	crossing	[27]
459	ܥܣܪܐ	num.	ten	[27]
460	ܦܬܓܡܐ	n. m.	word	[27]
461	ܫܘܩܐ	n. m.	bazaar, marketplace, square, street	[27]
462	ܫܘܬܦ	v.	be partaker	[27]
463	ܬܐܪܬܐ	n. f.	conscience	[27]
464	ܐܝܠܢܐ	n. m.	tree	[26]
465	ܐܝܡܟܐ	particle	whence?	[26]
466	ܙܩܝܦܐ	n. m.	cross, the Cross	[26]
467	ܟܪܡܐ	n. m.	vineyard	[26]
468	ܠܐܐ	v.	labour, toil; Af'el tire	[26]
469	ܡܟܣܐ	n. m.	publican, tax collector	[26]
470	ܥܕܪ	v.	advantage, help, be of profit	[26]
471	ܫܒܩ	v.	Af'el allow, permit	[26]
472	ܦܬܟܪܐ	n. m.	idol, image	[26]
473	ܩܒܪܐ	n. m.	grave, sepulchre, tomb	[26]
474	ܩܕܫ	v.	Pa''el consecrate, sanctify	[26]
475	ܪܓܝܓܬܐ	n. f.	lust	[26]
476	ܫܬܐ	num.	six	[26]
477	ܬܡܗ	v.	be astonished; Af'el astonish	[26]

Words occurring 25 times:

Ref.	Syriac	Cat.	Meaning	
478	ܐܟܚܕܐ	particle	as one, together	[25]
479	ܐܪܒܥܝܢ	num.	forty	[25]
480	ܐܫܕ	v.	pour out	[25]

Ref.	Syriac	Cat.	Meaning	
481	ܕܒܚܐ	n. m.	sacrifice, victim	[25]
482	ܕܟܝܐ	adj.	clean, pure	[25]
483	ܙܢܝܘܬܐ	n. f.	adultery, fornication, harlotry	[25]
484	ܝܣܦ	v.	Af˓el add, increase	[25]
485	ܟܠܐ	v.	hinder, restrain, forbid	[25]
486	ܡܐܐ	num.	one hundred	[25]
487	ܣܝܡܬܐ	n. f.	treasure, store	[25]
488	ܦܩܚܐ	adj.	better, expedient, profitable	[25]
489	ܩܢܛܪܘܢܐ	n. m.	Gr. κεντυρίων centurion	[25]

Words occurring 24 times:

Ref.	Syriac	Cat.	Meaning	
490	ܓܒܝܐ	pp.	approved, chosen, elect	[24]
491	ܕܒܪ	v.	Ethpa˓˓al be transmitted; Af˓el conduct, lead away, take	[24]
492	ܝܩܝܪܐ	adj.	heavy, precious	[24]
493	ܟܘܪܗܢܐ	n. m.	ailment, disease, infirmity, sickness	[24]
494	ܡܐܬܝܬܐ	n. f.	advent, coming	[24]
495	ܡܕܒܚܐ	n. m.	altar	[24]
496	ܡܚܘܬܐ	n. f.	plague, stroke, wound	[24]
497	ܥܕܢܐ	n. m.	moment, opportunity, season, time	[24]
498	ܥܕܥܐܕܐ	n. m.	feast, festival	[24]
499	ܨܘܡ	v.	fast	[24]
500	ܪܓ	v.	covet, desire, lust	[24]
501	ܫܘܓ	v.	Af˓el wash	[24]
502	ܫܘܒܗܪܐ	n. m.	glorying, vainglory, vaunting	[24]
503	ܫܬܩ	v.	keep silent, be still; Pa˓˓el silence	[24]

Words occurring 22 and 23 times:

Ref.	Syriac	Cat.	Meaning	
504	ܒܘܝܐܐ	n. m.	comfort, encouragement	[23]
505	ܟܐܢܐ	adj.	just, righteous, upright	[23]
506	ܡܚܫܒܬܐ	n. f.	thought, reasoning, counsel	[23]

Ref.	Syriac	Cat.	Meaning	
507	ܣܦܩ	v.	suffice, be able, be sufficient	[23]
508	ܚܪܒܐ	n. m.	sheep	[23]
509	ܦܘܪܩܢܐ	n. m.	deliverance, redemption, salvation	[23]
510	ܨܦܪܐ	n. m.	daybreak, morning	[23]
511	ܪܚܝܩܐ	adj.	distant, far, remote	[23]
512	ܬܝܒܘܬܐ	n. f.	repentance	[23]
513	ܬܟܠ	v.	Ethpᶜel be confident	[23]
514	ܒܝܬ	particle	among, between	[22]
515	ܒܪܝܬܐ	n. f.	creation	[22]
516	ܓܒܐ	n. m.	side, party, sect, part (of a ship),	[22]
517	ܗܟܘܬ	particle	likewise, so	[22]
518	ܚܕܪܐ	n. m.	circle, surroundings, vagrancy	[22]
519	ܚܪܝܢܐ	n. m.	altercation, contention, contradiction, dispute, strife	[22]
520	ܚܬܐ	n. f.	sister	[22]
521	ܛܥܡ	v.	partake (of), taste; Ethpᶜel be grafted; Afᶜel graft	[22]
522	ܛܡܪ	v.	hide oneself, be hidden; Paᶜᶜel hide	[22]
523	ܣܢܩ	v.	need	[22]
524	ܦܠܚܐ	n. m.	servant, worshipper, soldier	[22]
525	ܦܫܩ	v.	Paᶜᶜel expound, interpret	[22]
526	ܩܪܢܐ	n. f.	horn, corner	[22]
527	ܫܬܐܣܬܐ	n. f.	foundation	[22]
528	ܬܩܢ	v.	be restored; Paᶜᶜel prepare, restore; Afᶜel establish	[22]

Words occurring 21 times:

Ref.	Syriac	Cat.	Meaning	
529	ܐܒܕܢܐ	n. m.	loss, perdition, waste	[21]
530	ܐܣܛܪܛܝܘܛܐ	n. m.	Gr. στρατιώτης soldier	[21]
531	ܒܣܡܐ	n. m.	ointment, unguent, incense (censings)	[21]
532	ܒܩܐ	v.	examine, prove; Ethpaᶜᶜal consider	[21]
533	ܚܘܪܐ	adj.	white	[21]
534	ܚܣܝܪܐ	adj.	deficient, lacking	[21]
535	ܝܪܚܐ	n. m.	month	[21]
536	ܟܠܝܘܡ	idiom	everyday	[21]

Ref.	Syriac	Cat.	Meaning	
537	ܟܦܢ	v.	hunger	[21]
538	ܠܒܘܫܐ	n. m.	apparel, clothing, dress	[21]
539	ܡܟܝܟܐ	adj.	gentle, humble, lowly	[21]
540	ܢܘܟܪܝܐ	adj.	alien, foreign, strange	[21]
541	ܢܣܝܘܢܐ	n. m.	temptation, trial	[21]
542	ܢܨܪܝܐ	adj.	Nazarene	[21]
543	ܣܘܓܐܐ	n. m.	abundance, multitude	[21]
544	ܣܐܒ	v. Pa^{cc}el	defile	[21]
545	ܣܟܠܘܬܐ	n. f.	error, foolishness, wrong-doing	[21]
546	ܥܘܬܪܐ	n. m.	riches, wealth	[21]
547	ܦܨܐ	v. Pa^{cc}el	deliver	[21]
548	ܬܬܐ	n. f.	fig, fig tree	[21]

Words occurring 20 times:

Ref.	Syriac	Cat.	Meaning	
549	ܐܝܟܢܐ	particle	like as	[20]
550	ܐܣܘܪܐ	n. m.	bond, chain, fetter	[20]
551	ܐܪܡܝܐ	adj.	Aramaean (Syrian), Gentile	[20]
552	ܒܢܝܢܐ	n. m.	building, edification	[20]
553	ܚܕܝ	v.	be merry, be rejoice; Pa^{cc}el anoint; Ethpa^{cc}al live joyfully, live merrily	[20]
554	ܓܙܪ	v.	circumcise, cut	[20]
555	ܕܝܢܪܐ	n. m.	Gr. δηνάριον denarius	[20]
556	ܗܓܡܘܢܐ	n. m.	Gr. ἡγεμών governor, prefect	[20]
557	ܚܣܝܢܐ	adj.	mighty, potentate, robust, strong	[20]
558	ܚܠܝܡܐ	adj.	healthy, sound, strong, whole	[20]
559	ܚܠܦ	v.	Pa^{cc}el change, transmute; Šaf^{c}el alter, change	[20]
560	ܚܡܬܐ	n. f.	anger, fury, wrath	[20]
561	ܚܨܕ	v.	reap	[20]
562	ܟܕܘ	pron.	= ܟܕ + ܗܘ it suffices	[20]
563	ܟܠܝܪܟܐ	n. m.	Gr. χιλίαρχος captain of a thousand	[20]
564	ܡܬܘܡ	particle	always, ever	[20]
565	ܢܒܝܘܬܐ	n. f.	prophecy	[20]

Ref.	Syriac	Cat.	Meaning	
566	ܣܠܐ	v.	despise, reject	[20]
567	ܣܪܩ	v.	Pa``cc``el make *empty*, make *void*	[20]
568	ܥܘܪܠܘܬܐ	n. f.	uncircumcision	[20]
569	ܥܩܪܐ	n. m.	root	[20]
570	ܪܓܡ	v.	stone	[20]
571	ܪܥܝܐ	n. m.	pastor, shepherd	[20]
572	ܫܠܝ	v.	cease, be quiet; Pa``cc``el *quiet, stop*	[20]
573	ܫܡܪܝܐ	adj.	Samaritan	[20]

Words occurring 19 times:

574	ܐܟܠ ܩܪܨܐ	n.	accuser, calumniator	[19]
575	ܒܕܪ	v.	disperse, scatter, spend, waste, scare away	[19]
576	ܓܘܕܦܐ	n. m.	blasphemy	[19]
577	ܓܪ	v.	commit *adultery*	[19]
578	ܙܝܬܐ	n. m.	olive, w/ ܛܘܪ Mount of Olives	[19]
579	ܚܒܠܐ	n. m.	corruption, decay	[19]
580	ܚܦܛ	v.	Pa``cc``el encourage, exhort, incite	[19]
581	ܟܐܐ	v.	Pa``cc``el *rebuke*	[19]
582	ܟܠܝܠܐ	n. m.	crown, wreath	[19]
583	ܡܕܒܪܐ	n. m.	desert, wilderness	[19]
584	ܡܟ	v.	be humble; Pa``cc``el *humble*	[19]
585	ܥܠܝܡܐ	n. m.	young *man,* young *man, youth*	[19]
586	ܦܬܘܪܐ	n. m.	table	[19]
587	ܩܢܝܢܐ	n. m.	goods, possession, property, substance	[19]
588	ܩܪܒܐ	n. m.	battle, war, fighting	[19]
589	ܪܡܫܐ	n. m.	evening	[19]
590	ܪܥܐ	v.	feed, tend	[19]
591	ܫܒܛܐ	n. m.	rod, sceptre, staff, tribe, ܡܩܒܠ ܫܒܛܐ *magistrates*	[19]
592	ܫܘܒܩܢܐ	n. m.	forgiveness, release, remission, repudiation	[19]

Ref.	Syriac	Cat.	Meaning	
			Words occurring 17 and 18 times:	
593	ܒܘܪܟܬܐ	n. f.	benediction, blessing	[18]
594	ܕܪܟ	v.	Af`el comprehend, overtake	[18]
595	ܚܐܪܐ	adj.	free, freedman, noble	[18]
596	ܣܡܟ	denom.	Pa`el confirm, strengthen	[18]
597	ܚܨܐ	n. m.	back (of the body), loins	[18]
598	ܝܬܒ	v.	inherit	[18]
599	ܡܕܥܐ	n. m.	knowledge, mind, understanding	[18]
600	ܡܘܡܬܐ	n. f.	curse, oath	[18]
601	ܡܢܝܢܐ	n. m.	number	[18]
602	ܡܪܚ	denom.	Af`el dare	[18]
603	ܢܟܠܐ	n. m.	craft, deceit, guile, guilt, trickery	[18]
604	ܣܒܥ	v.	be full, be satisfied; Pa`el satisfy	[18]
605	ܣܟܠܐ	adj.	foolish	[18]
606	ܦܠܚܐ	n. m.	cultivator, husbandman, tiller	[18]
607	ܦܫܛ	v.	tr. stretch out; int. be straight	[18]
608	ܨܝܕ	particle	at, near, with	[18]
609	ܩܨܐ	v.	break (bread)	[18]
610	ܪܒܝ	n. m.	master, rabbi	[18]
611	ܪܓܬܐ	n. f.	desire, lust	[18]
612	ܫܕܪ	v.	send	[18]
613	ܐܘ	particle	O!, Oh!	[17]
614	ܒܨܪ	v.	decrease, be inferior, be less	[17]
615	ܓܢܒܐ	n. m.	thief	[17]
616	ܚܛܦ	v.	seize, snatch	[17]
617	ܝܪܬܘܬܐ	n. f.	inheritance	[17]
618	ܟܒܪ	particle	perhaps, long ago	[17]
619	ܟܝܢܐ	n. m.	nature	[17]
620	ܡܫܟܢܐ	n. m.	tabernacle, tent, habitation	[17]
621	ܥܛܦ	v.	turn; Pa`el clothe	[17]
622	ܪܫܐ	v.	Pa`el despise	[17]
623	ܡܛܐ	v.	obtain	[17]

Ref.	Syriac	Cat.	Meaning	
624	ܪܓܙ	v.	be angry; Af`el provoke	[17]
625	ܫܓܫ	v.	stir up, trouble	[17]
626	ܬܒܥ	v.	avenge, require	[17]
627	ܬܘܕܝܬܐ	n. f.	avowal, confession, thanksgiving	[17]

Words occurring 16 times:

628	ܚܣܕ	denom.	Pa``el deride, mock	[16]
629	ܠܒܣܬܪܐ	particle	the back, backwards, behind	[16]
630	ܚܕܕܐ	pron.	one another	[16]
631	ܚܣ	particle	let it not be, God forbid	[16]
632	ܚܣܡܐ	n. m.	envy, jealousy, emulation	[16]
633	ܚܪܫܐ	adj.	deaf, dumb, mute	[16]
634	ܚܫܐ	n. m.	suffering, feeling, passion, experience, lust	[16]
635	ܝܪܬܐ	n. m.	heir	[16]
636	ܟܝ	particle	indeed, now, perhaps	[16]
637	ܟܝܡ	particle	then, therefore	[16]
638	ܡܚܝܢܐ	adj.	life-giving, preserver, Saviour	[16]
639	ܡܢܘ	pron.	= ܡܢ + ܗܘ what is this?	[16]
640	ܡܢܬܐ	n. f.	part, portion	[16]
641	ܡܨܝܕܬܐ	n. f.	net	[16]
642	ܢܗܝܪܐ	adj.	bright, illumined, light, (pl.) luminaries	[16]
643	ܣܥܪܐ	n. m.	hair	[16]
644	ܥܢܐ	n. f.	flock	[16]
645	ܦܪܚܬܐ	n. f.	bird	[16]
646	ܩܒܪ	v.	bury; Pa``el heap up	[16]
647	ܪܒܘܬܐ	n. f.	greatness, constr. w/ ܟܘܡܪܐ high priesthood	[16]
648	ܫܘܡܠܝܐ	n. m.	consummation, end, fulfilment, fulness	[16]
649	ܫܘܬܦܘܬܐ	n. f.	communion, fellowship, participation, partnership	[16]
650	ܫܠܝܐ	n. m.	calm, cessation, lull, quietness, silence, w/ ܡܢ suddenly	[16]
651	ܫܢܩ	v.	Pa``el torment	[16]
652	ܫܪܓܐ	n. m.	lamp, light, wick	[16]

Word Frequency List: 653 - 680

Ref.	Syriac	Cat.	Meaning	

Words occurring 15 times:

Ref.	Syriac	Cat.	Meaning	
653	ܐܟܣܢܝܐ	adj.	Gr. ξένος guest, stranger	[15]
654	ܒܪܐ	v.	create, make	[15]
655	ܒܚܪܬܐ	particle	afterwards	[15]
656	ܓܢܒ	v.	steal	[15]
657	ܕܪܬܐ	n. f.	atrium, court	[15]
658	ܗܪ	v.	suffer harm; Af‹el harm, hurt	[15]
659	ܚܫܡܝܬܐ	n. f.	supper; pl. feasts	[15]
660	ܚܬܢܐ	n. m.	bridegroom	[15]
661	ܛܘܗܡܐ	n. m.	birth, family, kin, nationality	[15]
662	ܟܦܪ	v.	wrong, deny, reject	[15]
663	ܡܟܝܟܘܬܐ	n. f.	humility, lowliness, meekness, condescension	[15]
664	ܡܥܡܕܢܐ	n. m.	baptizer	[15]
665	ܢܗܪܐ	n. m.	river	[15]
666	ܨܗܐ	v.	be thirsty	[15]
667	ܨܠܡܐ	n. m.	figure, image, portrait	[15]
668	ܩܝܣܐ	n. m.	tree, wood	[15]
669	ܩܢܘܡܐ	n. m.	individual (self), person, substance	[15]
670	ܩܪܨܐ	n. m.	always w/ ܐܟܠ accuse	[15]
671	ܩܫܝܐ	adj.	hard, rough, strong	[15]
672	ܪܗܘܡܝܐ	adj.	Roman	[15]
673	ܪܘܚܩܐ	n. m.	w/ ܡܢ from afar, far place, far place	[15]
674	ܪܢܐ	v.	consider, meditate, plan, think	[15]
675	ܫܝܘܠ	n. f.	Sheol, place of the dead	[15]
676	ܬܕܡܘܪܬܐ	n. f.	wonder, marvel, prodigy	[15]
677	ܬܠܝܬܝܐ	n. m.	third	[15]
678	ܬܚܘܡܐ	n. m.	border, boundary, confine	[15]
679	ܬܫܥ	num.	nine	[15]

Words occurring 14 times:

Ref.	Syriac	Cat.	Meaning	
680	ܐܪܟܘܢܐ	n. m.	Gr. ἄρχων captain, magistrate, ruler	[14]

Ref.	Syriac	Cat.	Meaning	
681	ܒܘܪܟܐ	n. f.	knee	[14]
682	ܒܬܘܠܬܐ	n. f.	virgin	[14]
683	ܓܙܪܬܐ	n. f.	island	[14]
684	ܕܡܐ	n. m.	price	[14]
685	ܙܒܘܪܐ	n. m.	bowl, platter	[14]
686	ܙܕܘܩܝܐ	adj.	Sadducee	[14]
687	ܙܕܩܬܐ	n. f.	alms, almsgiving, charity	[14]
688	ܚܕܪ	v.	wander, surround, beg; Af'el hedge	[14]
689	ܚܙܝܪܐ	n. m.	swine	[14]
690	ܚܠܡ	v.	Ethp'el be cured; Af'el cure	[14]
691	ܚܡܝܪܐ	n. m.	leaven	[14]
692	ܚܣܪ	v.	lack, lose	[14]
693	ܚܪܒܐ	n. c.	sword, slaughter, ploughshare	[14]
694	ܛܢܦܘܬܐ	n. f.	impurity, uncleaness	[14]
695	ܝܠܘܕܐ	n. m.	babe, child, infant	[14]
696	ܟܐܒܐ	n. m.	disease, pain, suffering	[14]
697	ܟܘܒܐ	n. m.	thorn	[14]
698	ܟܦܢܐ	n. m.	famine, hunger	[14]
699	ܡܘܡܐ	n. m.	blemish, spot	[14]
700	ܡܨܐ	v.	be able	[14]
701	ܡܫܚ	v.	anoint	[14]
702	ܡܫܚܐ	n. m.	oil, ointment, unguent	[14]
703	ܡܫܪܝܐ	pp.	paralytic	[14]
704	ܡܫܬܘܬܐ	n. f.	wedding feast, festivity, symposium	[14]
705	ܣܝܦܐ	n. m.	sword	[14]
706	ܣܟܠ	denom.	Af'el offend, wrong	[14]
707	ܣܡܟܐ	n. m.	company at a meal, feast, seat at a meal	[14]
708	ܣܦܪܐ	n. m.	book, roll, scroll	[14]
709	ܥܘܠܐ	adj.	wicked, unjust	[14]
710	ܦܠܐܬܐ	n. f.	comparison, parable	[14]
711	ܩܕܝܫܘܬܐ	n. f.	holiness, sanctification	[14]
712	ܫܘܥܐ	n. m.	rock	[14]
713	ܫܘܬܦܐ	n. m.	partaker, partner	[14]

Ref.	Syriac	Cat.	Meaning	
714	ܫܝܢܐ	n. m.	peace, tranquility	[14]
715	ܫܢܐ	n. f.	tooth, tusk, ivory	[14]
716	ܫܩܐ	v.	Af`el give to drink, water	[14]
717	ܬܘܩܠܐ	n. f.	offense, stumbling block	[14]
718	ܬܘܪܐ	n. m.	ox, steer	[14]
719	ܬܢܝܢܐ	n. m.	dragon, monster	[14]
720	ܗܐ	particle	here	[14]
721	ܬܪܥܝܬܐ	n. f.	mind, thought, imagination	[14]

Words occurring 13 times:

Ref.	Syriac	Cat.	Meaning	
722	ܒܝܫܘܬܐ	n. f.	wickedness, wrong-doing	[13]
723	ܚܣܐ	v.	despise; Af`el despise, neglect	[13]
724	ܚܢܝܢܘܬܐ	n. f.	gentleness, gladness, kindliness, pleasantness	[13]
725	ܕܪܫ	v.	argue, debate, dispute, question; Pa``el train	[13]
726	ܙܘܥܐ	n. m.	agitation, commotion, earthquake, shaking	[13]
727	ܝܒܒ	v.	cry out	[13]
728	ܚܘܝܐ	n. m.	serpent	[13]
729	ܚܣܝܪܘܬܐ	n. f.	defect, need, want	[13]
730	ܚܣܢ	v.	Ethp`el affirm, argue, contend, hold on to, strive	[13]
731	ܚܪܪ	v.	Pa``el set free	[13]
732	ܚܫܚ	v.	be useful; Ethpa``al adapt, apply, use	[13]
733	ܛܒܥܐ	n. m.	seal, stamp	[13]
734	ܡܐܢ	v.	tedious, be tired, be weary; Af`el neglect	[13]
735	ܡܫܘܚܬܐ	n. f.	measure, proportion	[13]
736	ܢܨܒ	v.	plant	[13]
737	ܢܫܩ	v.	kiss	[13]
738	ܣܘܟܐ	n. f.	branch	[13]
739	ܣܘܥܪܢܐ	n. m.	affair, deed, event, happening, matter, visitation	[13]
740	ܣܝܒܪܬܐ	n. f.	food, sustenance	[13]
741	ܣܡܠܐ	n. f.	left	[13]
742	ܥܒܕܘܬܐ	n. f.	bondage, service	[13]
743	ܥܝܠܐ	n. m.	colt, young animal	[13]

Ref.	Syriac	Cat.	Meaning	
744	ܥܡܠܐ	n. m.	labour, toil	[13]
745	ܦܥܠܐ	n. m.	labourer, worker	[13]
746	ܩܝܡܐ	adj.	abiding, lasting, remaining, valid	[13]
747	ܪܛܢ	v.	murmur	[13]
748	ܪܫܝܢܐ	n. m.	blame, accusation, w/ ܕܠܐ blameless	[13]
749	ܫܓܘܫܝܐ	n. m.	commotion, riot, tumult, uproar	[13]
750	ܫܘܘܕܝܐ	n. m.	promise	[13]
751	ܬܪܢܓܠܐ	n. m.	cock	[13]

Words occurring 12 times:

752	ܐܣܟܡܐ	n. m.	Gr. σχῆμα fashion, figure, form	[12]
753	ܒܝܫܐܝܬ	adv.	badly, sorely	[12]
754	ܒܠܥ	v.	swallow up, be beaten, be smitten, be struck	[12]
755	ܒܥܘܬܐ	n. f.	petition, prayer	[12]
756	ܒܪܝܐ	adj.	outer	[12]
757	ܕܢܚ	v.	dawn, rise, shine; Af'el make rise	[12]
758	ܙܢܝܬܐ	n. f.	harlot, prostitute	[12]
759	ܙܩܐ	n. f.	leather bag, wineskin	[12]
760	ܚܛܐ	n. f.	wheat	[12]
761	ܚܢܦܐ	adj.	foreigner, godless, heathen, profane, Gentile	[12]
762	ܚܢܩ	v.	choke, strangle; Pa''el drown	[12]
763	ܚܨܕܐ	n. m.	harvest	[12]
764	ܛܢ	v.	be eager, be jealous; Af'el provoke jealousy	[12]
765	ܛܢܢܐ	n. m.	jealousy, zeal	[12]
766	ܝܒܠ	v.	bear, carry; Af'el make carry	[12]
767	ܝܒܫ	v.	dry up, wither; Af'el cause to wither	[12]
768	ܝܕܝܥܐ	pp.	apparent, certain (one), known, notable	[12]
769	ܝܘܬܪܢܐ	n. m.	abundance, advantage, gain, lucre, profit	[12]
770	ܝܠܕܐ	n. m.	birth, fruit (of the vine), offspring	[12]
771	ܝܫܛ	v.	Af'el stretch out	[12]
772	ܟܟܪܐ	n. f.	talent	[12]
773	ܟܣܣ	v.	Ethp'el be reproved; Af'el admonish, convict, rebuke	[12]

Ref.	Syriac	Cat.	Meaning	
774	ܡܚܐ	v.	fight, strike; Ethpa``c``cal endeavor, strive	[12]
775	ܡܓܕܠܝܬܐ	adj.	Magdelene	[12]
776	ܡܚܪ	adv.	tomorrow	[12]
777	ܡܛܪܐ	n. m.	rain	[12]
778	ܡܟܐ	particle	= ܡܢ + ܟܐ, of time: *from this time*, ܡܟܐ ܘܡܟܐ *here and there*	[12]
779	ܡܢܪܬܐ	n. f.	candlestick, lamp-stand	[12]
780	ܡܣܒܐ	n. m.	acceptance, taking, constr. w/ ܐܦ̈ܐ *hypocrisy*	[12]
781	ܢܓܕ	v.	Af``c``el make *long*, w/ ܪܘܚܐ *be patient, be prolonged*	[12]
782	ܢܝܚܬܐ	n. f.	leisure, recreation, repose, rest	[12]
783	ܩܕܠܐ	particle	before	[12]
784	ܥܝܕܐ	n. m.	custom, manner	[12]
785	ܥܬܝܩܐ	adj.	ancient, old	[12]
786	ܥܬܪ	v.	grow *rich*; Af``c``el make *rich*	[12]
787	ܦܠܓܘܬܐ	n. f.	division, portion, separation	[12]
788	ܩܛܝܪܐ	n. m.	force, necessity, violence	[12]
789	ܩܢܝܐ	n. m.	cane, pen, reed	[12]
790	ܩܪܝܐ	pp.	called, being by vocation	[12]
791	ܪܒܘܬܐ	n. f.	myriad, ten thousand	[12]
792	ܪܥܡܐ	n. m.	thunder	[12]
793	ܫܘܪܝܐ	n. m.	beginning	[12]
794	ܫܫܠܬܐ	n. f.	chain	[12]
795	ܬܡܢܝܐ	num.	eight	[12]
796	ܬܢܢܐ	n. m.	smoke	[12]

Words occurring 11 times:

Ref.	Syriac	Cat.	Meaning	
797	ܐܚܝܕܐ	pp.	holder, closed	[11]
798	ܐܚܪ	v.	Af``c``el delay, tarry	[11]
799	ܐܪܥ	v.	encounter, meet	[11]
800	ܒܗܬܬܐ	n. f.	shame	[11]
801	ܒܡ	n. f.	Gr. βῆμα judgement-seat, tribunal	[11]
802	ܓܗܢܐ	n.	hell, Gehenna	[11]

Ref.	Syriac	Cat.	Meaning	
803	ܚܲܡܝܼܡܵܐ	pp.	mature, perfect	[11]
804	ܕܲܣܡܵܐ	n. m.	attendant, guard, officer, servant	[11]
805	ܕܸܟܪܵܐ	adj.	male	[11]
806	ܕܸܡܥܬܵܐ	n. f.	tear	[11]
807	ܗܘܼܦܵܟܵܐ	n. m.	behaviour, conduct, manner of life, ways	[11]
808	ܚܣ	v.	pity, spare	[11]
809	ܚܢܵܢܵܐ	n. m.	compassion, favour, mercy	[11]
810	ܚܫܸܟ	v.	grow dark; Af'el darken; Ettaf'al be darkened	[11]
811	ܛܲܡܐܵܐ	adj.	impure, unclean	[11]
812	ܝܵܐܝܵܐ	adj.	becoming, congruous, decorous, due, seemly	[11]
813	ܝܲܡܬܵܐ	n. f.	lake	[11]
814	ܟܵܐ	particle	here	[11]
815	ܟܘܼܬܝܼܢܵܐ	n. f.	coat, linen garment, tunic	[11]
816	ܟܬܵܢܵܐ	n. m.	linen sheet	[11]
817	ܟܬܪ	v.	Pa''el abide, continue, remain, wait	[11]
818	ܡܓܝܼܪܵܢܘܼܬܵܐ	n. f.	long suffering	[11]
819	ܡܠܟܵܐ	n. m.	counsel	[11]
820	ܡܲܦܩܵܐ	n. m.	answer, constr. w/ ܪܘܼܚܵܐ defense	[11]
821	ܡܫܲܚܠܦܵܐ	pp.	different, diverse, various	[11]
822	ܡܬܘܿܡ	particle	always, ever	[11]
823	ܢܩܫ	v.	knock	[11]
824	ܣܩܘܼܒܠܵܐ	adj.	adverse, contrary	[11]
825	ܣܪܝܼܩܵܐ	pp.	empty, vacant, vain, void	[11]
826	ܥܒܪܵܐܝܬ	adv.	in Aramaic, only in Rev. in Hebrew	[11]
827	ܥܡܘܿܪܵܐ	n. m.	dweller, inhabitant	[11]
828	ܥܣܪܝܼܢ	num.	twenty	[11]
829	ܦܵܪܘܿܩܵܐ	n. m.	deliverer, Saviour	[11]
830	ܦܨܐ	v.	burst, rend; Ethpa''al w/ ܥܠ break out against	[11]
831	ܩܛܠܵܐ	n. m.	murder, slaughter	[11]
832	ܩܝܼܢܕܘܼܢܘܿܣ	n. f.	Gr. κίνδυνος danger, peril	[11]
833	ܩܲܪܩܦܬܵܐ	n. f.	head, skull	[11]
834	ܪܗܒ	v.	Ethp'el be frightened; Saf'el hurry	[11]
835	ܪܟܒ	v.	mount, ride; Ethpa''al be constructed; Af'el make ride	[11]

Ref.	Syriac	Cat.	Meaning	
836	ܪܰܫܺܝܥܳܐ	adj.	impious, ungodly, wicked	[11]
837	ܬܠܳܬܺܝܢ	num.	thirty	[11]

Words occurring 10 times:

838	ܐܓܽܘܢܳܐ	n. m.	Gr. ἀγών conflict, contest	[10]
839	ܐܶܓܳܪܳܐ	n. m.	housetop, roof	[10]
840	ܐܶܡܘܳܬܳܐ	n. c.	nation, people	[10]
841	ܐܰܣܢܳܐ	adj.	cousin, kinsman; f. kinswoman	[10]
842	ܐܰܝܟܐ	particle	= ܐܰܝܟܳܐ + ܗܽܘ where is (he)?	[10]
843	ܐܰܡܺܝܢܳܐ	adj.	constant	[10]
844	ܐܰܡܺܝܢܳܐܺܝܬ	adv.	assiduously, constantly	[10]
845	ܐܰܡܬܳܐ	n. f.	handmaid, female bond- servant	[10]
846	ܒܚܰܪ	v.	examine, search	[10]
847	ܓܠܺܝܠܳܝܳܐ	adj.	Galilean	[10]
848	ܓܥܠ	denom.	Ethpᶜel be entrusted; Afᶜel commend, commit	[10]
849	ܕܓܶܠ	v.	Paᶜᶜel lie, speak falsely	[10]
850	ܕܳܫ	v.	trample	[10]
851	ܕܥܶܟ	v.	extinguish, go out (fire); Paᶜᶜel quench	[10]
852	ܙܰܢܳܝܳܐ	adj.	adulterer, fornicator	[10]
853	ܚܺܐܪܽܘܬܳܐ	n. f.	freedom, liberty	[10]
854	ܚܰܣܺܝܢܳܐ	adj.	mighty, strong	[10]
855	ܚܦܺܝܛܽܘܬܳܐ	n. f.	diligence, earnestness, perseverance, zest	[10]
856	ܚܬܰܡ	v.	impress, seal, stamp	[10]
857	ܛܽܘܥܝܰܝ	n. f.	deception, error, mistake	[10]
858	ܝܰܒܫܳܐ	n. m.	earth, dry land	[10]
859	ܝܰܘܢܳܐ	n. c.	dove	[10]
860	ܟܢܳܬܳܐ	n. m.	companion, fellow servant	[10]
861	ܟܽܘܪܗܳܢܳܐ	n. f.	frailty, infirmity, sickness, weakness	[10]
862	ܟܰܪܝܽܘܬܳܐ	n. f.	sadness, sorrowfulness	[10]
863	ܠܒܒ	denom.	Paᶜᶜel encourage	[10]
864	ܠܘܺܝ	v.	Paᶜᶜel escort	[10]
865	ܡܗܰܝܡܢܳܐ	n. m.	eunuch, faithful	[10]

Ref.	Syriac	Cat.	Meaning	
866	ܡܢܝܐ	n. m.	mina (monetary unit)	[10]
867	ܡܣܢܐ	n. m.	sandal, shoe	[10]
868	ܡܥܕܪܢܐ	n. m.	help, helper	[10]
869	ܡܩܕܘܢܝܐ	adj.	Macedonian	[10]
870	ܡܫܠܡܢܐ	n. m.	betrayer, traitor	[10]
871	ܡܫܡܥܬܐ	n. f.	hearing, obedience	[10]
872	ܡܫܪܝܬܐ	n. f.	encampment	[10]
873	ܣܐܡܐ	n. m.	Gr. ἄσημον *money, silver*	[10]
874	ܣܗܪܐ	n. c.	moon	[10]
875	ܣܝܦܐ	n. f.	sword	[10]
876	ܣܪܝܩܐܝܬ	adv.	vainly	[10]
877	ܥܘܡܩܐ	n. m.	deep, depth	[10]
878	ܥܪܛܠܝܐ	adj.	bare, naked, exposed	[10]
879	ܦܘܠܚܢܐ	n. m.	work, occupation, trade	[10]
880	ܦܠܓܐ	n. m.	half, middle	[10]
881	ܨܚܝ	v.	Pa``el *revile*	[10]
882	ܩܛܪܓ	v.	Gr. κατηγορεῖν *accuse*	[10]
883	ܩܨܝܐ	n. m.	fragment	[10]
884	ܩܪܝܢܐ	n. m.	calling, lesson, reading, vocation	[10]
885	ܪܘܝ	v.	become *drunk*	[10]
886	ܪܟܫܐ	n. m.	horse	[10]
887	ܪܩܕ	v.	dance; Af`el *mourn*	[10]
888	ܫܛ	v.	treat w/ *contempt, despise*	[10]
889	ܬܘܟܠܢܐ	n. m.	confidence, trust	[10]
890	ܬܩܠ	v.	hinder, stumble	[10]
891	ܬܪܣܝ	v.	feed, nourish, support	[10]

Section 2:
Proper Noun Frequency List

Sequence.

This list is arranged according to the frequency of occurrence of proper nouns.

Format.

The list consists of four columns:

- Column 1: Sequential No.
  Gives a sequential number.

- Column 2: Syriac Lexical Entry.
  Gives the Syriac form of the proper noun in vocalized *Serto* (Western) script.

- Column 3: Category.
  Gives the grammatical category (always pr. n.) of the lexical entry.

- Column 4: English Meanings.
  Gives the English meanings of the lexical entry. Main English key words are given in italic. At the right side of this column, the frequency of the lexical entry is given in italic between square brackets, [ ].

The list is divided into frequency-range parts to help the student plan study sessions.

How to Use the Frequency List.

Same as Section 1.

No.	Syriac	Cat.	Meaning	
			Words occurring 141 - 1113 times:	
1	ܝܫܘܥ	pr. n.	Jesus	[1113]
2	ܦܘܠܘܣ	pr. n.	Paul	[171]
3	ܐܘܪܫܠܡ	pr. n.	Jerusalem	[143]
4	ܫܡܥܘܢ	pr. n.	Simon (Peter)	[141]
			Words occurring 49 - 95 times:	
5	ܝܘܚܢܢ	pr. n.	John (the Baptist)	[95]
6	ܟܐܦܐ	pr. n.	Cephas	[89]
7	ܡܘܫܐ	pr. n.	Moses	[82]
8	ܐܝܣܪܐܝܠ	pr. n.	Israel	[77]
9	ܐܒܪܗܡ	pr. n.	Abraham	[75]
10	ܓܠܝܠܐ	pr. n.	Galilee	[63]
11	ܕܘܝܕ	pr. n.	David	[60]
12	ܦܝܠܛܘܣ	pr. n.	Pontius Pilate	[58]
13	ܝܗܘܕ	pr. n.	Judea	[49]
			Words occurring 20 - 35 times:	
14	ܝܘܚܢܢ	pr. n.	John (the disciple)	[35]
15	ܩܣܪ	pr. n.	Gr. καῖσαρ Caesar	[35]
16	ܐܠܝܐ	pr. n.	Elijah	[31]
17	ܒܪܢܒܐ	pr. n.	Barnabas	[28]
18	ܗܪܘܕܣ	pr. n.	Herod Antipas	[26]
19	ܝܘܣܦ	pr. n.	Joseph (Mary's husband)	[25]
20	ܝܥܩܘܒ	pr. n.	Jacob	[25]
21	ܡܨܪܝܢ	pr. n.	Egypt	[25]
22	ܛܝܡܬܐܘܣ	pr. n.	Timotheus	[24]
23	ܝܗܘܕܐ	pr. n.	Judas (Iscariot)	[24]
24	ܫܐܘܠ	pr. n.	Saul	[23]
25	ܐܫܥܝܐ	pr. n.	Isaiah	[22]

No.	Syriac	Cat.	Meaning	
26	ܝܥܩܘܒ	pr. n.	James (John's brother)	[21]
27	ܐܝܣܚܩ	pr. n.	Isaac	[20]
28	ܡܪܝܡ	pr. n.	Mary (Jesus' mother)	[20]

Words occurring 15 - 19 times:

29	ܐܣܝܐ	pr. n.	Asia	[19]
30	ܡܩܕܘܢܝܐ	pr. n.	Macedonia	[18]
31	ܐܦܣܘܣ	pr. n.	Ephesus	[16]
32	ܟܦܪܢܚܘܡ	pr. n.	Capernaum	[16]
33	ܦܝܠܝܦܘܣ	pr. n.	Philip (the apostle)	[16]
34	ܕܪܡܣܘܩ	pr. n.	Damascus	[15]
35	ܝܘܪܕܢܢ	pr. n.	Jordan	[15]
36	ܩܣܪܝܐ	pr. n.	Caesarea	[15]

Words occurring 12 - 14 times:

37	ܐܓܪܦܘܣ	pr. n.	Agrippa	[14]
38	ܐܢܛܝܟܝܐ	pr. n.	Antioch of Syria	[14]
39	ܛܛܘܣ	pr. n.	Titus	[14]
40	ܡܪܝܡ	pr. n.	Mary (Magdalene)	[14]
41	ܦܗܣܛܘܣ	pr. n.	(Porcius) Festus	[14]
42	ܦܝܠܝܦܘܣ	pr. n.	Philip (one of the seven)	[14]
43	ܐܢܕܪܐܘܣ	pr. n.	Andrew	[13]
44	ܒܝܬ ܥܢܝܐ	pr. n.	Bethany	[13]
45	ܗܪܘܕܣ	pr. n.	Herod the Great	[13]
46	ܡܪܝܡ	pr. n.	Mary (Lazarus' sister)	[13]
47	ܡܪܬܐ	pr. n.	Martha	[13]
48	ܢܨܪܬ	pr. n.	Nazareth	[13]
49	ܫܝܠܐ	pr. n.	Silas	[13]
50	ܒܒܠ	pr. n.	Babylon	[12]
51	ܙܒܕܝ	pr. n.	Zebedee	[12]
52	ܣܟܪܝܘܛܐ	pr. n.	Iscariot	[12]

No.	Syriac	Cat.	Meaning	
53	ܫܠܝܡܘܢ	pr. n.	Solomon	[12]

Words occurring 10 and 11 times:

54	ܐܟܐܝܐ	pr. n.	Achaia	[11]
55	ܒܪ ܐܒܐ	pr. n.	Barabbas	[11]
56	ܙܟܪܝܐ	pr. n.	Zacharias (John's father)	[11]
57	ܠܥܙܪ	pr. n.	Lazarus (of Bethany)	[11]
58	ܨܘܪ	pr. n.	Tyre	[11]
59	ܨܝܕܢ	pr. n.	Sidon	[11]
60	ܬܐܘܡܐ	pr. n.	Thomas	[11]
61	ܐܠܝܫܒܥ	pr. n.	Elizabeth	[10]
62	ܐܦܠܘ	pr. n.	Apollos	[10]
63	ܝܥܩܘܒ	pr. n.	James (Jesus' brother)	[10]
64	ܡܠܟܝܙܕܩ	pr. n.	Melchisedec	[10]
65	ܣܕܘܡ	pr. n.	Sodom	[10]
66	ܩܝܦܐ	pr. n.	Caiaphas	[10]

Section 3:
Greek Frequency List

Sequence.

This list is arranged according to the frequency of occurrence of Syriac words derived from Greek.

Format.

The list consists of four columns:

- **Column 1: Sequential No.**
  Gives a sequential number.

- **Column 2: Syriac Lexical Entry.**
  Gives the Syriac form of the word in vocalized *Serto* (Western) script.

- **Column 3: Category.**
  Gives the grammatical category of the lexical entry.

- **Column 4: Greek Form and English Meanings.**
  Gives the Greek form followed by the English meanings of the lexical entry. At the right side of this column, the frequency of the lexical entry is given in italic between square brackets, [ ].

How to Use the Frequency List.

Same as Section 1.

No.	Syriac	Cat.	Meaning	
1	ܓܝܪ	particle	Gr. γάρ *for*	[1085]
2	ܢܡܘܣܐ	n. m.	Gr. νόμος *law*	[224]
3	ܦܝܣ	denom.	Gr. πεῖσαι Af\`el *convince, persuade*	[66]
4	ܦܪܨܘܦܐ	n. m.	Gr. πρόσωπον *aspect, countenance, face, person*	[35]
5	ܩܣܪ	pr. n.	Gr. καῖσαρ *Caesar*	[35]
6	ܕܝܬܩܐ	n. f.	Gr. διαθήκη *covenant, testament*	[31]
7	ܐܘܢܓܠܝܘܢ	n. m.	Gr. εὐαγγέλιον *Gospel*	[30]
8	ܩܢܛܪܘܢܐ	n. m.	Gr. κεντυρίων *centurion*	[25]
9	ܐܣܛܪܛܝܘܛܐ	n. m.	Gr. στρατιώτης *soldier*	[21]
10	ܕܝܢܪܐ	n. m.	Gr. δηνάριον *denarius*	[20]
11	ܗܓܡܘܢܐ	n. m.	Gr. ἡγεμών *governor, prefect*	[20]
12	ܟܠܝܪܟܐ	n. m.	Gr. χιλίαρχος *captain of a thousand*	[20]
13	ܐܟܣܢܝܐ	adj.	Gr. ξένος *guest, stranger*	[15]
14	ܐܪܟܘܢܐ	n. m.	Gr. ἄρχων *captain, magistrate, ruler*	[14]
15	ܐܣܟܡܐ	n. m.	Gr. σχῆμα *fashion, figure, form*	[12]
16	ܒܝܡ	n. f.	Gr. βῆμα *judgement-seat, tribunal*	[11]
17	ܩܝܢܕܘܢܘܣ	n. f.	Gr. κίνδυνος *danger, peril*	[11]
18	ܐܓܘܢܐ	n. m.	Gr. ἀγών *conflict, contest*	[10]
19	ܐܣܡܐ	n. m.	Gr. ἄσημον *money, silver*	[10]
20	ܩܛܪܓ	v.	Gr. κατηγορεῖν *accuse*	[10]

Section 4:
Consonantal Homographs

Sequence.

This list is arranged in alphabetical order.

Format.

The list consists of four columns:

- Column 1: Sequential No.
  Gives a sequential number.

- Column 2: Syriac Lexical Entry.
  Gives the Syriac form of the word in vocalized *Serto* (Western) script.

- Column 3: Category.
  Gives the grammatical category of the lexical entry.

- Column 4: English Meanings.
  Gives the English meanings of the lexical entry. Main English key words are given in italic. At the right side of this column, the frequency of the lexical entry is given in italic between square brackets, [ ].

A horizontal line divides the pairs of homographs.

How to Use the Homograph List.

The student should pay attention to the vocalization, for it is the only way, in most cases, to distinguish between each pair of consonantal homographs. Note that some pairs belong to different grammatical categories. In most pairs there is one entry whose frequency is much higher than the other. It is worth while remembering which one is more frequent.

Notice that in verbal forms, the following pairs are consonantal homographs:

- Perfect sing. 3 masc., and active participle sing. 3 masc.
- Perfect sing. 3 fem., sing. 2 masc., and sing. 1 com.

Also notice that in verbal forms, the following are identical homographs:

- Imperfect: sing. 3 masc. and pl. 1 com.
- Imperfect: sing. 3 fem. and sing 2 masc.

For examples, see the tables in Section 6.

No.	Syriac	Cat.	Meaning	
1	ܐܰܓܪܳܐ	n. m.	pay, recompense, reward	[31]
2	ܐܶܓܳܪܳܐ	n. m.	housetop, roof	[10]
3	ܐܘ	particle	O!, Oh!	[17]
4	ܐܘ	particle	else, or, rather than	[296]
5	ܐܰܠܦܳܐ	num.	thousand	[48]
6	ܐܶܠܦܳܐ	n. f.	boat, ship	[45]
7	ܐܳܬܳܐ	n. f.	*miraculous* token, sign	[82]
8	ܐܳܬܳܐ	v.	come; Af^cel bring	[966]
9	ܒܪܳܐ	n. m.	son	[786]
10	ܒܪܳܐ	v.	create, make	[15]
11	ܓܒܳܐ	v.	choose, collect (tribute or tax), elect; Pa^{cc}el *gather*	[44]
12	ܓܰܒܳܐ	n. m.	part (of a ship), party, sect, side	[22]
13	ܕܝܢܳܐ	n. m.	judgement, sentence (of judge)	[101]
14	ܕܰܝܳܢܳܐ	n. m.	judge	[27]
15	ܕܡܳܐ	n. m.	blood	[96]
16	ܕܡܳܐ	v.	resemble; Pa^{cc}el compare, liken to	[70]
17	ܗܘ	pron.	he, (as enclitic) is, it	[1792]
18	ܗܘ	pron.	that, those, w/ ܕ he who	[1256]
19	ܚܝܳܐ	v.	live; Af^cel *make* live, save	[165]
20	ܚܰܝܳܐ	adj.	alive, living	[89]
21	ܚܰܝܶܐ	n. m.	life, salvation	[177]
22	ܚܠܦ	v.	Pa^{cc}el change, transmute; Šaf^cel alter, change	[20]

No.	Syriac	Cat.	Meaning	
23	ܚܠܦ	particle	for, instead	[117]
24	ܝܡܐ	v.	take an *oath*, *swear*; Af`el make *swear*	[34]
25	ܝܡܐ	n. m.	sea	[108]
26	ܟܣܐ	n. m.	cup	[33]
27	ܟܣܐ	v.	conceal, cover, hide	[31]
28	ܡܗܝܡܢܐ	n. m.	eunuch, faithful	[10]
29	ܡܗܝܡܢܐ	n. m.	believer, believing	[46]
30	ܡܠܟܐ	n. m.	king; f. queen	[130]
31	ܡܠܟܐ	n. m.	counsel	[11]
32	ܡܢ	pron.	w/ ܕ he who, who	[367]
33	ܡܢ	particle	from	[2966]
34	ܡܢܘ	pron.	= ܡܢ + ܗܘ who is this?	[126]
35	ܡܢܘ	pron.	= ܡܢܐ + ܗܘ what is this?	[16]
36	ܣܒܪ	v.	consider, suppose, think; Pa``el hope	[108]
37	ܣܒܪ	denom.	Pa``el declare, preach; Pai`el bear, endure; Ethpai`al be fed	[113]
38	ܣܟܠ	v.	Pa``el make *understand*; Ethpa``al *understand*	[49]
39	ܣܟܠ	denom.	Af`el offend, wrong	[14]
40	ܣܦܪܐ	n. m.	book, roll, scroll	[14]
41	ܣܦܪܐ	n. m.	lawyer, scribe	[76]
42	ܥܒܕܐ	n. m.	servant	[141]
43	ܥܒܕܐ	n. m.	deed, work	[191]
44	ܥܘܠܐ	adj.	unjust, wicked	[14]

No.	Syriac	Cat.	Meaning	
45	ܥܰܘ̈ܠܳܐ	n. m.	iniquity, unrighteousness	[39]
46	ܥܰܠ	v.	enter; Af'el bring in	[264]
47	ܥܰܠ	particle	about, concerning, on	[1549]
48	ܥܢܳܐ	v.	answer	[158]
49	ܥܳܢܳܐ	n. f.	flock	[16]
50	ܦܳܠܚܳܐ	n. m.	servant, soldier, worshipper	[22]
51	ܦܰܠܳܚܳܐ	n. m.	cultivator, husbandman, tiller	[18]
52	ܩܕܰܡ	v.	go before	[52]
53	ܩܕܳܡ	particle	before	[290]
54	ܪܰܒ	adj.	chief, great, w/ suffix master	[395]
55	ܪܒܳܐ	v.	grow up, increase; Pa''el cause increase, nourish	[35]
56	ܪܶܒܽܘܬܳܐ	n. f.	myriad, ten thousand	[12]
57	ܪܰܒܽܘܬܳܐ	n. f.	greatness, constr. w/ ܟܳܗܢܽܘܬܳܐ high priesthood	[16]
58	ܪܳܚܡܳܐ	n. m.	friend	[29]
59	ܪܰܚܡܳܐ	n. m.	bowels, mercy	[39]
60	ܪܳܡܳܐ	adj.	high, w/ ܩܳܠ loud voice	[39]
61	ܪܡܳܐ	v.	cast, place, put	[136]
62	ܪܥܳܐ	v.	feed, tend	[19]
63	ܪܥܳܐ	denom.	Ethpa''al think	[43]
64	ܫܶܢܳܐ	n. f.	ivory, tooth, tusk	[14]
65	ܫܢܳܐ	v.	be mad; Pa''el depart, remove	[35]

Section 5:
Verbal Forms

Sequence.

This list is arranged in the order of verbal morphological forms as described under *Preliminaries* below.

Format.

The list consists of four columns:

- **Column 1: Reference No.**
  Gives a cross reference to the corresponding lexical entry in Section 1.

- **Column 2: Perfect.**
  Gives the 'perfect' form of the verb in question in vocalized *Serto* (Western) script.

- **Column 3: Imperfect.**
  Gives the 'imperfect' form of the verb in question in vocalized *Serto* (Western) script.

- **Column 4: Notes.**
  At the right side of this column, the frequency of the lexical entry is given in italic between square brackets, [ ].

How to Use the List of Verbal Forms.

First read the next section, *Preliminaries*, very carefully. It is recommended that the student consult the grammars regarding the subject of verbal forms (specially how the imperfect is derived from the perfect). Any of the following readings will be useful (see the Bibliography for full reference details):

- Muraoka, *Classical Syriac*, §41 and §42 ff.
- Robinson, *Paradigms and Exercises in Syriac Grammar*, §15 and §16.

The only way to know the form of the imperfect is by referring to the lexicon. It is therefore recommended to study each verb entry as a pair (perfect → imperfect).

Preliminaries

Verbs, in terms of their consonantal roots, are classified as follows:

- Strong: any verb which does not fit any of the remaining categories.
- Initial *nun*: verbs whose first radical is a *nun*.
- Double: verbs whose second and third radicals are the same (in general the third radical is not written).
- Weak: verbs where at least one of the radicals is a weak letter (*alaph*, *waw* or *yudh*). If the first radical is *alaph*, the verb is called 'initial *alaph*'; if the middle radical is *yudh*, the verb is called 'middle *yudh*', and so on.

Under each of the above categories, verbs are classified according to the vowel which the second radical of the 'perfect' takes, and the vowel which the second radical of the 'imperfect' takes. For example, the strong verb can take *a* or *e* as the vowel of the second radical in the perfect, and *a*, *e* or *u* in the imperfect.

Verbal Forms

Ref.	Perfect	Imperfect	Notes

Strong with Final Guttural. perf. 2nd rad. ՚ – impf. 2nd rad. ՚ :

Ref.	Perfect	Imperfect	Notes	
162	ܗܓܰܕ݂	ܢܗܓܰܕ݂		[108]
163	ܕܓܰܕ݂	ܢܕܓܰܕ݂		[108]
42	ܥܩܰܒ݂	ܢܥܩܰܒ݂		[448]
38	ܥܒܰܕ݂	ܢܥܒܶܕ݂	See Section 6, Tables 13-14.	[494]

Strong. perf. 2nd rad. ՚ – impf. 2nd rad. ՝ :

Ref.	Perfect	Imperfect	Notes	
31	ܕܒܰܪ	ܢܕܒܰܪ	See Section 6, Tables 1-5.	[706]

Strong. perf. 2nd rad. ՚ – impf. 2nd rad. ՝ :

Ref.	Perfect	Imperfect	Notes	
84	ܢܓܰܕ݂	ܢܓܕ݂ܘܢ	See Section 6, Table 6.	[231]
137	ܩܦܰܝ	ܢܩܦܘܢ		[130]
98	ܡܓܰܠ	ܢܡܓܠܘܢ		[200]
145	ܨܠܰܝ	ܢܨܠܘܢ		[124]
92	ܡܓܶܕ݂	ܢܡܓܕ݂ܘܢ		[217]
119	ܥܩܰܠ	ܢܥܩܠܘܢ		[160]

Strong. perf. 2nd rad. ՝ – impf. 2nd rad. ՚ :

Ref.	Perfect	Imperfect	Notes	
155	ܫܺܟܠ	ܬܺܫܟܠ		[114]
151	ܗܨܶܦ	ܢܗܨܶܦ		[118]
149	ܕܣܶܡ	ܢܕܣܶܡ		[119]
99	ܡܟܶܡ	ܢܡܟܶܡ	See Section 6, Tables 7-10.	[200]

Strong. perf. 2nd rad. ՝ – impf. 2nd rad. ՝ :

Ref.	Perfect	Imperfect	Notes	
77	ܡܶܕ݂	ܢܡܕ݂ܘܢ	See Section 6, Tables 11-12.	[244]

Ref.	Perfect	Imperfect	Notes	

Strong verbs not used in P^{c}al:

158	ܒܿܟܼܪ	ܢܒܿܟܼܪ	= Pa^{cc}el.	[110]
148	ܒܠܲܥ		Used only as pass. part. in P^{c}al.	[120]
82	ܒܿܙܼܙ	ܢܒܿܙܼܙ	= Pa^{cc}el.	[235]

Initial ܒ . perf. 2nd rad. ´ - impf. 2nd rad. ˇ :

136	ܒܲܓ݂ܢ	ܢܲܒ݂ܓ݂ܢ		[130]
85	ܒܼܗܼܬ	ܢܒ݂ܗܼܬ	See Section 6, Table 15.	[229]

Initial ܒ . perf. 2nd rad. ´ - impf. 2nd rad. ˆ :

121	ܒܩܼܠ	ܢܒ݂ܩܿܠ	See Section 6, Table 16.	[157]

Initial ܒ . perf. 2nd rad. ´ - impf. 2nd rad. ʿ :

49	ܒܥܼܐ	ܢܒ݂ܥܸܐ	See Section 6, Tables 17-18.	[405]

Initial ܒ . perf. 2nd rad. ˆ - impf. 2nd rad. ʿ :

161	ܒܣܸܡ	ܢܒ݂ܣܲܡ	See Section 6, Table 19.	[108]

Double:

55	ܡܿܬܼܠ	ܢܡܿܬܿܠ	See Section 6, Tables 20-21.	[350]
73	ܓܼܠ	ܢܬܿܘܸܠ	See Section 6, Tables 22-23.	[264]

Initial ܐ . perf. 2nd rad. ´ - impf. 2nd rad. ´ :

43	ܐܼܙܲܠ	ܢܼܐܙܲܠ		[447]
5	ܐܼܡܲܪ	ܢܼܐܡܲܪ	See Section 6, Table 24.	[2551]

Ref.	Perfect	Imperfect	Notes

Initial ܠ . perf. 2nd rad. ´ - impf. 2nd rad. ˊ :

112	ܠܳܒܶܫ	ܢܶܠܒܰܫ		[168]
106	ܠܐܶܟ	ܢܶܠܐܟ	See Section 6, Table 25.	[178]

Middle ܠ :

79	ܥܰܠܠ	ܢܶܥܰܠܠ	See Section 6, Tables 26-28.	[243]

Final ܠ :

59	ܚܟܰܠ	ܢܶܚܟܰܠ		[313]
28	ܫܐܶܠ	ܢܶܫܐܶܠ	See Section 6, Tables 29-30.	[734]
116	ܨܠܳܠ	ܢܶܨܠܳܠ		[166]
120	ܚܢܰܠ	ܢܶܚܢܰܠ		[158]
69	ܪܓܰܠ	ܢܶܪܓܰܠ		[273]
175	ܐܳܠ	ܢܐܳܠ		[100]
56	ܥܕܰܠ	ܢܶܥܕܰܠ		[330]
76	ܥܕܰܠ	ܢܶܥܕܰܠ		[249]

Initial and Final ܠ :

18	ܠܐܶܠ	ܢܶܠܐܶܠ	See Section 6, Tables 31-32.	[966]

Initial ܢ . perf. 2nd rad. ´ - impf. 2nd rad. ´ :

32	ܢܒܰܣ	ܢܶܒܰܣ	See Section 6, Tables 33-36.	[704]

Initial ܢ . perf. 2nd rad. ˆ - impf. 2nd rad. ´ :

147	ܢܟܶܣ	ܢܶܟܰܣ		[120]
129	ܢܟܽܣ	ܢܶܟܽܣ	See Section 6, Tables 37-38.	[147]

Ref.	Perfect	Imperfect	Notes	

Initial ܝ . perf. 2nd rad. ˚ - impf. 2nd rad. ˚ :

126	ܝܬܒ	ܢܬܒ	See Section 6, Table 39.	[148]

Middle ܝ :

117	ܣܐܡ	ܢܣܝܡ	See Section 6, Tables 40-41.	[165]
94	ܫܐܡ	ܢܫܝܡ	See Section 6, Tables 42-43.	[207]

Middle ܘ :

110	ܩܡ	ܢܩܘܡ		[171]
36	ܡܝܬ	ܢܡܘܬ	See Section 6, Tables 44-45.	[550]

Other verbal forms:

62	ܐܘܫܛ	ܢܘܫܛ	See Section 6, Table 50.	[305]
37	ܐܙܠ	ܢܐܙܠ	See Section 6, Tables 46—47.	[534]
134	ܗܠܟ	ܢܗܠܟ	See Section 6, Tables 48-49.	[134]

Section 6:
Verbal Paradigms

Sequence.

The tables are arranged in the order of verbal morphological forms as described under *Preliminaries* in Section 5.

Format.

- The header of each table indicates the verbal category from Section 5, followed by the verb conjugated in the tables. The 'No.' in the header gives the verb's reference number in Section 1.
- Each table consists of five columns and ten rows. The columns indicate tense, and the rows indicate number, person and gender.
- The tail of each table gives the infinitive.
- Three horizontal lines in the table, '---', indicate that the verb does not exist for that particular set of number, person and gender.
  Forms which do not occur in the Syriac New Testament for the cited verb are also included since they may occur for other verbs of the same category; these forms are marked with an asterisk, '*'
- Only the most frequent verb of each category in Section 5 is fully conjugated.

How to Use the Verbal Paradigms.

It is recommended that the student consult the grammars regarding the subject of verbal paradigms. Any of the following readings will be useful (see the Bibliography for full reference details):

- Healey, *First Studies*, sections iv and vii ff., and tables on pp. 80-107.
- Muraoka, *Classical Syriac*, §41-§55, and tables on p. 103 ff.
- Nöldeke, *Compendious Syriac Grammar*, §158 ff.
- Robinson, *Paradigms and Exercises in Syriac Grammar*, p. 54 ff.

Index to the Lists of Paradigms.

Note that the following conjugated frequent verbs do not occur in the Syriac New Testament in all possible forms. The following index can be used for finding the paradigm of a particular form.

I. Strong Verbs.
- P'al Forms:
  - Perfect: *a* in 2nd radical, Tables 1, 6.
  - Perfect: *e* in 2nd radical, Tables 7, 11.
  - Imperfect: *a* in 2nd radical, Table 7.

- Imperfect: *e* in 2nd radical, Table 1
- Imperfect: *u* in 2nd radical, Tables 6, 11
- Ethp'el Forms:
  - Perfect: *e* in 2nd radical, Tables 2, 8.
  - Imperfect: *e* in 2nd radical, Tables 2, 8.
  - *š* as 1st radical, Table 8.
- Pa''el Forms: Table 9.
- Ethpa''al Forms:
  - Tables 10, 12.
  - *š* as 1st radical, Table 10.
- Af'el Forms: Table 3.
- Šaf'el Forms: Table 4.
- Eštaf'al Forms: Table 5.

II. Final Guttural (*'ain*):

- P'al Forms: Table 13.
- Ethp'el Forms: Table 14.

III. Initial *nun* Verbs.

- P'al Forms:
  - Perfect: *a* in 2nd radical, Tables 15, 16, 17.
  - Perfect: *e* in 2nd radical, Table 19.
  - Imperfect: *a* in 2nd radical, Table 15.
  - Imperfect: *e* in 2nd radical, Table 16.
  - Imperfect: *u* in 2nd radical, Tables 17, 19.
- Af'el Forms: Table 18.

IV. Double Verbs.

- P'al Forms: Tables 22.
- Pa''el Forms: Table 20.
- Ethpa''al Forms: Table 21.
- Af'el Forms: Table 23.

V. Initial *Aleph* Verbs.

- P'al Forms:
  - Perfect: *a* in 2nd radical, Tables 24, 25.
  - Imperfect: *a* in 2nd radical, Table 24.
  - Imperfect: *u* in 2nd radical, Table 25.

VI. Middle *Aleph* Verbs.

- P'al Forms: Table 26.
- Ethp'el Forms with initial *š*: Table 27.
- Pa''el Forms: Table 28.

VII. Final *Aleph* Verbs.
- P'al Forms: Tables 29, 31.
- Ethp'el Forms: Table 30.
- Af'el Forms: Table 32.

VIII. Initial *Yudh* Verbs.
- P'al Forms: Tables 33, 37, 39.
- Ethp'el Forms: Table 34.
- Pa"el Forms: Table 38.
- Af'el Forms: Table 35.
- Eštaf'al Forms: Table 36.

IX. Middle *Yudh* Verbs:
- P'al Forms: Tables 40, 42.
- Af'el Forms: Tables 41, 43.

X. Middle *Waw* Verbs.
- P'al Forms: Table 44.
- Af'el Forms: Table 45.

XI. Anomalous Verbs.
- Tables 46-50.

TABLE 1. Strong. perf. 2nd rad. ́ – impf. 2nd rad. ̂ : the verb ܚܓܪ, No. 31

Form: Pᶜal	Perfect	Imperfect	Imperative	Act. Part.	Pass. Part.
sing. 3 masc.	ܚܓܰܪ	ܢܶܚܓܽܘܪ	---	ܚܳܓܰܪ	ܚܓܺܝܪ
sing. 3 fem.	ܚܶܓܪܰܬ݀	ܬܶܚܓܽܘܪ	---	ܚܳܓܪܳܐ	ܚܓܺܝܪܳܐ
sing. 2 masc.	ܚܓܰܪܬ	ܬܶܚܓܽܘܪ	ܚܓܽܘܪ	---	---
sing. 2 fem.	* ܚܓܰܪܬܝ	* ܬܶܚܓܪܺܝܢ	* ܚܓܽܘܪܝ	---	---
sing. 1 com.	ܚܶܓܪܶܬ݀	ܐܶܚܓܽܘܪ	---	---	---
pl. 3 masc.	ܚܓܰܪܘ	ܢܶܚܓܪܽܘܢ	---	ܚܳܓܪܺܝܢ	ܚܓܺܝܪܺܝܢ
pl. 3 fem.	* ܚܓܰܪ	* ܢܶܚܓܪܳܢ	---	ܚܳܓܪܳܢ	* ܚܓܺܝܪܳܢ
pl. 2 masc.	ܚܓܰܪܬܽܘܢ	ܬܶܚܓܪܽܘܢ	ܚܓܽܘܪܘ	---	---
pl. 2 fem.	* ܚܓܰܪܬܶܝܢ	* ܬܶܚܓܪܳܢ	* ܚܓܽܘܪܶܝܢ	---	---
pl. 1 com.	ܚܓܰܪܢ	ܢܶܚܓܽܘܪ	---	---	---
Infinitive:	* ܡܶܚܓܰܪ				

Note. In late Western Syriac, pl. 3 f. is ܚܓܰܪܝ̈.

TABLE 2.

Form: Ethpᶜel	Perfect	Imperfect	Imperative	Act. Part.	Pass. Part.
sing. 3 masc.	ܐܶܬܚܓܰܪ	* ܢܶܬܚܓܰܪ	---	---	* ܡܶܬܚܓܰܪ
sing. 3 fem.	* ܐܶܬܚܰܓܪܰܬ݀	* ܬܶܬܚܓܰܪ	---	---	* ܡܶܬܚܰܓܪܳܐ
sing. 2 masc.	* ܐܶܬܚܓܰܪܬ	* ܬܶܬܚܓܰܪ	* ܐܶܬܚܓܰܪ	---	---
sing. 2 fem.	* ܐܶܬܚܓܰܪܬܝ	* ܬܶܬܚܰܓܪܺܝܢ	* ܐܶܬܚܰܓܪܝ	---	---
sing. 1 com.	* ܐܶܬܚܓܪܶܬ݀	* ܐܶܬܚܓܰܪ	---	---	---
pl. 3 masc.	* ܐܶܬܚܓܰܪܘ	* ܢܶܬܚܰܓܪܽܘܢ	---	---	* ܡܶܬܚܰܓܪܺܝܢ
pl. 3 fem.	* ܐܶܬܚܓܰܪ	* ܢܶܬܚܰܓܪܳܢ	---	---	* ܡܶܬܚܰܓܪܳܢ
pl. 2 masc.	* ܐܶܬܚܓܰܪܬܽܘܢ	* ܬܶܬܚܰܓܪܽܘܢ	* ܐܶܬܚܰܓܪܘ	---	---
pl. 2 fem.	* ܐܶܬܚܓܰܪܬܶܝܢ	* ܬܶܬܚܰܓܪܳܢ	* ܐܶܬܚܰܓܪܶܝܢ	---	---
pl. 1 com.	* ܐܶܬܚܓܰܪܢ	* ܢܶܬܚܓܰܪ	---	---	---
Infinitive:	* ܡܶܬܚܰܓܪܽܘ				

TABLE 3.

Form: Afᶜel	Perfect	Imperfect	Imperative	Act. Part.	Pass. Part.
sing. 3 masc.	* ܐܲܚܬܸܡ	* ܢܲܚܬܸܡ	---	ܡܲܚܬܸܡ	* ܡܲܚܬܸܡ
sing. 3 fem.	ܐܲܚܬܡܲܬ	* ܬܲܚܬܸܡ	---	* ܡܲܚܬܡܵܐ	ܡܲܚܬܡܵܐ
sing. 2 masc.	* ܐܲܚܬܸܡܬ	* ܬܲܚܬܸܡ	* ܐܲܚܬܸܡ	---	---
sing. 2 fem.	* ܐܲܚܬܸܡܬܝ	* ܬܲܚܬܡܝܼܢ	* ܐܲܚܬܸܡܝ	---	---
sing. 1 com.	ܐܲܚܬܡܹܬ	* ܐܲܚܬܸܡ	---	---	---
pl. 3 masc.	* ܐܲܚܬܸܡܘ	ܢܲܚܬܡܘܼܢ	---	* ܡܲܚܬܡܝܼܢ	* ܡܲܚܬܡܝܼܢ
pl. 3 fem.	* ܐܲܚܬܸܡ	ܢܲܚܬܡܵܢ	---	* ܡܲܚܬܡܵܢ	* ܡܲܚܬܡܵܢ
pl. 2 masc.	* ܐܲܚܬܸܡܬܘܿܢ	* ܬܲܚܬܡܘܼܢ	* ܐܲܚܬܸܡܘ	---	---
pl. 2 fem.	* ܐܲܚܬܸܡܬܹܝܢ	* ܬܲܚܬܡܵܢ	* ܐܲܚܬܸܡܝ	---	---
pl. 1 com.	* ܐܲܚܬܸܡܢ	* ܢܲܚܬܸܡ	---	---	---
Infinitive:	* ܡܲܚܬܵܡܘܿ				

TABLE 4.

Form: Šafᶜel	Perfect	Imperfect	Imperative	Act. Part.	Pass. Part.
sing. 3 masc.	ܫܲܚܬܸܡ	ܢܫܲܚܬܸܡ	---	ܡܫܲܚܬܸܡ	ܡܫܲܚܬܸܡ
sing. 3 fem.	* ܫܲܚܬܡܲܬ	* ܬܫܲܚܬܸܡ	---	* ܡܫܲܚܬܡܵܐ	* ܡܫܲܚܬܡܵܐ
sing. 2 masc.	ܫܲܚܬܸܡܬ	* ܬܫܲܚܬܸܡ	* ܫܲܚܬܸܡ	---	---
sing. 2 fem.	* ܫܲܚܬܸܡܬܝ	* ܬܫܲܚܬܡܝܼܢ	* ܫܲܚܬܸܡܝ	---	---
sing. 1 com.	ܫܲܚܬܡܹܬ	* ܐܫܲܚܬܸܡ	---	---	---
pl. 3 masc.	* ܫܲܚܬܸܡܘ	ܢܫܲܚܬܡܘܼܢ	---	* ܡܫܲܚܬܡܝܼܢ	ܡܫܲܚܬܡܝܼܢ
pl. 3 fem.	ܫܲܚܬܸܡ	ܬܫܲܚܬܡܵܢ	---	* ܡܫܲܚܬܡܵܢ	ܡܫܲܚܬܡܵܢ
pl. 2 masc.	* ܫܲܚܬܸܡܬܘܿܢ	* ܬܫܲܚܬܡܘܼܢ	* ܫܲܚܬܸܡܘ	---	---
pl. 2 fem.	* ܫܲܚܬܸܡܬܹܝܢ	* ܬܫܲܚܬܡܵܢ	* ܫܲܚܬܸܡܝ	---	---
pl. 1 com.	ܫܲܚܬܸܡܢ	ܢܫܲܚܬܸܡ	---	---	---
Infinitive:	* ܡܫܲܚܬܵܡܘܿ				

Verbal Paradigms

TABLE 5.

Form: Eštaf ͨal	Perfect	Imperfect	Imperative	Act. Part.	Pass. Part.
sing. 3 masc.	ܐܫܬܰܥܒܰܕ	ܢܶܫܬܰܥܒܰܕ	---	---	ܡܫܬܰܥܒܰܕ
sing. 3 fem.	ܐܫܬܰܥܒܕܰܬ	ܬܶܫܬܰܥܒܰܕ	---	---	ܡܫܬܰܥܒܕܳܐ
sing. 2 masc.	* ܐܫܬܰܥܒܰܕܬ	* ܬܶܫܬܰܥܒܰܕ	* ܐܫܬܰܥܒܰܕ	---	---
sing. 2 fem.	* ܐܫܬܰܥܒܰܕܬܝ	* ܬܶܫܬܰܥܒܕܺܝܢ	* ܐܫܬܰܥܒܰܕܝ	---	---
sing. 1 com.	* ܐܫܬܰܥܒܕܶܬ	* ܐܫܬܰܥܒܰܕ	---	---	---
pl. 3 masc.	ܐܫܬܰܥܒܰܕܘ	ܢܶܫܬܰܥܒܕܘܢ	---	---	ܡܫܬܰܥܒܕܺܝܢ
pl. 3 fem.	* ܐܫܬܰܥܒܰܕ	ܢܶܫܬܰܥܒܕܳܢ	---	---	ܡܫܬܰܥܒܕܳܢ
pl. 2 masc.	* ܐܫܬܰܥܒܰܕܬܘܢ	ܬܶܫܬܰܥܒܕܘܢ	ܐܫܬܰܥܒܰܕܘ	---	---
pl. 2 fem.	* ܐܫܬܰܥܒܰܕܬܝܢ	* ܬܶܫܬܰܥܒܕܳܢ	* ܐܫܬܰܥܒܰܕܝܢ	---	---
pl. 1 com.	* ܐܫܬܰܥܒܰܕܢ	ܢܶܫܬܰܥܒܰܕ	---	---	---

Infinitive: * ܡܫܬܰܥܒܳܕܘ

TABLE 6. Strong. perf. 2nd rad. ́ – impf. 2nd rad. ̊ : the verb ܣܓܕ, No. 84

Form: P ͨal	Perfect	Imperfect	Imperative	Act. Part.	Pass. Part.
sing. 3 masc.	ܣܓܶܕ	* ܢܶܣܓܘܕ	---	ܣܳܓܶܕ	ܣܓܺܝܕ
sing. 3 fem.	* ܣܶܓܕܰܬ	* ܬܶܣܓܘܕ	---	* ܣܳܓܕܳܐ	ܣܓܺܝܕܳܐ
sing. 2 masc.	* ܣܓܶܕܬ	ܬܶܣܓܘܕ	ܣܓܘܕ	---	---
sing. 2 fem.	ܣܶܓܕܬܝ	ܬܶܣܓܕܺܝܢ	* ܣܓܘܕܝ	---	---
sing. 1 com.	ܣܶܓܕܶܬ	ܐܶܣܓܘܕ	---	---	---
pl. 3 masc.	ܣܓܶܕܘ	* ܢܶܣܓܕܘܢ	---	* ܣܳܓܕܺܝܢ	ܣܓܺܝܕܺܝܢ
pl. 3 fem.	ܣܓܶܕ	ܬܶܣܓܕܳܢ	---	* ܣܳܓܕܳܢ	ܣܓܺܝܕܳܢ
pl. 2 masc.	ܣܓܶܕܬܘܢ	ܬܶܣܓܕܘܢ	* ܣܓܘܕܘ	---	---
pl. 2 fem.	* ܣܓܶܕܬܝܢ	* ܬܶܣܓܕܳܢ	* ܣܓܘܕܝܢ	---	---
pl. 1 com.	ܣܓܶܕܢ	ܢܶܣܓܘܕ	---	---	---

Infinitive: * ܡܣܓܰܕ

Other Forms. Ethp ͨel = ܐܶܣܬܓܶܕ, same as ܐܶܬܟܬܶܒ (Table 2). Af ͨel occurs in ܢܰܣܓܕܘܢ (impf. pl. 3 m.) and ܡܰܣܓܶܕ (act. part. s. m.), (Table 3).

TABLE 7. Strong. perf. 2nd rad. ˚ – impf. 2nd rad. ´ : the verb ܡܟܡ , No. 99

Form: Pᶜal	Perfect	Imperfect	Imperative	Act. Part.	Pass. Part.
sing. 3 masc.	ܡܟܡ	ܢܡܟܡ	---	ܡܳܟܶܡ	* ܡܟܺܝܡ
sing. 3 fem.	* ܡܶܟܡܰܬ݂	ܬܶܡܟܰܡ	---	ܡܳܟܡܳܐ	* ܡܟܺܝܡܳܐ
sing. 2 masc.	* ܡܟܰܡܬ݁	* ܬܶܡܟܰܡ	* ܡܟܰܡ	---	---
sing. 2 fem.	* ܡܟܰܡܬ݁ܝ	* ܬܶܡܟܡܺܝܢ	* ܡܟܰܡܝ	---	---
sing. 1 com.	* ܡܶܟܡܶܬ݂	* ܐܶܡܟܰܡ	---	---	---
pl. 3 masc.	ܡܟܰܡܘ	ܢܶܡܟܡܽܘܢ	---	ܡܳܟܡܺܝܢ	* ܡܟܺܝܡܺܝܢ
pl. 3 fem.	ܡܟܰܡ	ܬܶܡܟܡܳܢ	---	ܡܳܟܡܳܢ	* ܡܟܺܝܡܳܢ
pl. 2 masc.	* ܡܟܰܡܬ݁ܘܢ	* ܬܶܡܟܡܽܘܢ	* ܡܟܰܡܘ	---	---
pl. 2 fem.	* ܡܟܰܡܬܶܝܢ	* ܬܶܡܟܡܳܢ	* ܡܟܰܡܶܝܢ	---	---
pl. 1 com.	* ܡܟܰܡܢ	ܢܶܡܟܰܡ	---	---	---
Infinitive:	* ܡܶܡܟܰܡ				

TABLE 8.

Form: Ethpᶜel	Perfect	Imperfect	Imperative	Act. Part.	Pass. Part.
sing. 3 masc.	ܐܶܬ݂ܡܟܶܡ	ܢܶܬ݂ܡܟܶܡ	---	---	ܡܶܬ݂ܡܟܶܡ
sing. 3 fem.	* ܐܶܬ݂ܡܰܟܡܰܬ݂	* ܬܶܬ݂ܡܟܶܡ	---	---	* ܡܶܬ݂ܡܟܡܳܐ
sing. 2 masc.	* ܐܶܬ݂ܡܟܶܡܬ݁	* ܬܶܬ݂ܡܟܶܡ	* ܐܶܬ݂ܡܟܶܡ	---	---
sing. 2 fem.	* ܐܶܬ݂ܡܟܶܡܬ݁ܝ	* ܬܶܬ݂ܡܟܡܺܝܢ	* ܐܶܬ݂ܡܟܶܡܝ	---	---
sing. 1 com.	ܐܶܬ݂ܡܟܡܶܬ݂	ܐܶܬ݂ܡܟܶܡ	---	---	---
pl. 3 masc.	ܐܶܬ݂ܡܟܶܡܘ	ܢܶܬ݂ܡܟܡܽܘܢ	---	---	* ܡܶܬ݂ܡܟܡܺܝܢ
pl. 3 fem.	* ܐܶܬ݂ܡܟܶܡ	ܬܶܬ݂ܡܟܡܳܢ	---	---	* ܡܶܬ݂ܡܟܡܳܢ
pl. 2 masc.	* ܐܶܬ݂ܡܟܶܡܬ݁ܘܢ	* ܬܶܬ݂ܡܟܡܽܘܢ	* ܐܶܬ݂ܡܟܶܡܘ	---	---
pl. 2 fem.	* ܐܶܬ݂ܡܟܶܡܬܶܝܢ	* ܬܶܬ݂ܡܟܡܳܢ	* ܐܶܬ݂ܡܟܶܡܶܝܢ	---	---
pl. 1 com.	ܐܶܬ݂ܡܟܶܡܢ	* ܢܶܬ݂ܡܟܶܡ	---	---	---
Infinitive:	* ܡܶܬ݂ܡܟܳܡܽܘ				

TABLE 9.

Form: Pa^{cc}el	Perfect	Imperfect	Imperative	Act. Part.	Pass. Part.
sing. 3 masc.	ܩܰܛܶܠ	ܢܩܰܛܶܠ	---	ܡܩܰܛܶܠ	ܡܩܰܛܰܠ
sing. 3 fem.	* ܩܰܛܠܰܬ݂	* ܬܩܰܛܶܠ	---	ܡܩܰܛܠܳܐ	* ܡܩܰܛܰܠܬܳܐ
sing. 2 masc.	ܩܰܛܶܠܬ	* ܬܩܰܛܶܠ	ܩܰܛܶܠ	---	---
sing. 2 fem.	* ܩܰܛܶܠܬܝ	* ܬܩܰܛܠܺܝܢ	* ܩܰܛܶܠܝ	---	---
sing. 1 com.	ܩܰܛܠܶܬ݂	ܐܩܰܛܶܠ	---	---	---
pl. 3 masc.	ܩܰܛܶܠܘ	* ܢܩܰܛܠܽܘܢ	---	ܡܩܰܛܠܺܝܢ	* ܡܩܰܛܠܺܝܢ
pl. 3 fem.	ܩܰܛܶܠ	ܬܩܰܛܠܳܢ	---	ܡܩܰܛܠܳܢ	* ܡܩܰܛܠܳܢ
pl. 2 masc.	* ܩܰܛܶܠܬܘܢ	* ܬܩܰܛܠܽܘܢ	ܩܰܛܶܠܘ	---	---
pl. 2 fem.	* ܩܰܛܶܠܬܶܝܢ	* ܬܩܰܛܠܳܢ	ܩܰܛܶܠܶܝܢ	---	---
pl. 1 com.	* ܩܰܛܶܠܢ	ܢܩܰܛܶܠ	---	---	---
Infinitive:	* ܡܩܰܛܳܠܽܘ				

TABLE 10.

Form: Ethpa^{cc}al	Perfect	Imperfect	Imperative	Act. Part.	Pass. Part.
sing. 3 masc.	ܐܶܬ݂ܩܰܛܰܠ	ܢܶܬ݂ܩܰܛܰܠ	---	---	ܡܶܬ݂ܩܰܛܰܠ
sing. 3 fem.	* ܐܶܬ݂ܩܰܛܠܰܬ݂	ܬܶܬ݂ܩܰܛܰܠ	---	---	* ܡܶܬ݂ܩܰܛܠܳܐ
sing. 2 masc.	* ܐܶܬ݂ܩܰܛܰܠܬ	* ܬܶܬ݂ܩܰܛܰܠ	* ܐܶܬ݂ܩܰܛܰܠ	---	---
sing. 2 fem.	* ܐܶܬ݂ܩܰܛܰܠܬܝ	* ܬܶܬ݂ܩܰܛܠܺܝܢ	* ܐܶܬ݂ܩܰܛܠܝ	---	---
sing. 1 com.	* ܐܶܬ݂ܩܰܛܠܶܬ݂	* ܐܶܬ݂ܩܰܛܰܠ	---	---	---
pl. 3 masc.	* ܐܶܬ݂ܩܰܛܰܠܘ	* ܢܶܬ݂ܩܰܛܠܽܘܢ	---	---	* ܡܶܬ݂ܩܰܛܠܺܝܢ
pl. 3 fem.	ܐܶܬ݂ܩܰܛܶܠ	* ܬܶܬ݂ܩܰܛܠܳܢ	---	---	ܡܶܬ݂ܩܰܛܠܳܢ
pl. 2 masc.	* ܐܶܬ݂ܩܰܛܰܠܬܘܢ	* ܬܶܬ݂ܩܰܛܠܽܘܢ	* ܐܶܬ݂ܩܰܛܠܘ	---	---
pl. 2 fem.	* ܐܶܬ݂ܩܰܛܰܠܬܶܝܢ	* ܬܶܬ݂ܩܰܛܠܳܢ	* ܐܶܬ݂ܩܰܛܠܶܝܢ	---	---
pl. 1 com.	ܐܶܬ݂ܩܰܛܰܠܢ	ܢܶܬ݂ܩܰܛܰܠ	---	---	---
Infinitive:	* ܡܶܬ݂ܩܰܛܳܠܽܘ				

Other Forms. Af^{c}el occurs in ܐܰܩܛܶܠ (perf. s. 3 m.), see Table 3.

TABLE 11. **Strong.** perf. 2nd rad. ܰ - impf. 2nd rad. ܘܽ : the verb ܩܪܰܒ , No. 77

Form: P^c^al	*Perfect*	*Imperfect*	*Imperative*	*Act. Part.*	*Pass. Part.*
sing. 3 masc.	ܩܪܰܒ	ܢܶܩܪܽܘܒ	---	ܩܳܪܶܒ	* ܩܪܺܝܒ
sing. 3 fem.	ܩܶܪܒܰܬ	* ܬܶܩܪܽܘܒ	---	* ܩܳܪܒܳܐ	* ܩܪܺܝܒܳܐ
sing. 2 masc.	* ܩܪܰܒܬ	ܬܶܩܪܽܘܒ	* ܩܪܽܘܒ	---	---
sing. 2 fem.	* ܩܪܰܒܬܝ	* ܬܶܩܪܒܺܝܢ	* ܩܪܽܘܒܝ	---	---
sing. 1 com.	* ܩܶܪܒܶܬ	* ܐܶܩܪܽܘܒ	---	---	---
pl. 3 masc.	ܩܪܰܒܘ	ܢܶܩܪܒܽܘܢ	---	ܩܳܪܒܺܝܢ	* ܩܪܺܝܒܺܝܢ
pl. 3 fem.	ܩܪܰܒܝ	* ܢܶܩܪܒܳܢ	---	* ܩܳܪܒܳܢ	* ܩܪܺܝܒܳܢ
pl. 2 masc.	* ܩܪܰܒܬܽܘܢ	* ܬܶܩܪܒܽܘܢ	ܩܪܽܘܒܘ	---	---
pl. 2 fem.	* ܩܪܰܒܬܶܝܢ	* ܬܶܩܪܒܳܢ	* ܩܪܽܘܒܶܝܢ	---	---
pl. 1 com.	* ܩܪܰܒܢ	ܢܶܩܪܽܘܒ	---	---	---
	Infinitive:	* ܡܶܩܪܰܒ			

Other Forms. Pa^cc^el = ܩܰܪܶܒ, same as ܩܰܕܶܡ (Table 9).

TABLE 12.

Form: Ethpa^cc^al	*Perfect*	*Imperfect*	*Imperative*	*Act. Part.*	*Pass. Part.*
sing. 3 masc.	ܐܶܬܩܰܪܰܒ	ܢܶܬܩܰܪܰܒ	---	---	ܡܶܬܩܰܪܰܒ
sing. 3 fem.	ܐܶܬܩܰܪܒܰܬ	ܬܶܬܩܰܪܰܒ	---	---	ܡܶܬܩܰܪܒܳܐ
sing. 2 masc.	* ܐܶܬܩܰܪܰܒܬ	* ܬܶܬܩܰܪܰܒ	ܐܶܬܩܰܪܰܒ	---	---
sing. 2 fem.	* ܐܶܬܩܰܪܰܒܬܝ	ܬܶܬܩܰܪܒܺܝܢ	* ܐܶܬܩܰܪܰܒܝ	---	---
sing. 1 com.	* ܐܶܬܩܰܪܒܶܬ	* ܐܶܬܩܰܪܰܒ	---	---	---
pl. 3 masc.	ܐܶܬܩܰܪܰܒܘ	ܢܶܬܩܰܪܒܽܘܢ	---	---	ܡܶܬܩܰܪܒܺܝܢ
pl. 3 fem.	* ܐܶܬܩܰܪܰܒ	* ܢܶܬܩܰܪܒܳܢ	---	---	* ܡܶܬܩܰܪܒܳܢ
pl. 2 masc.	ܐܶܬܩܰܪܰܒܬܽܘܢ	ܬܶܬܩܰܪܒܽܘܢ	* ܐܶܬܩܰܪܰܒܘ	---	---
pl. 2 fem.	* ܐܶܬܩܰܪܰܒܬܶܝܢ	* ܬܶܬܩܰܪܒܳܢ	* ܐܶܬܩܰܪܰܒܶܝܢ	---	---
pl. 1 com.	ܐܶܬܩܰܪܰܒܢ	ܢܶܬܩܰܪܰܒ	---	---	---
	Infinitive:	* ܡܶܬܩܰܪܳܒܽܘ			

Af^c^el = ܐܰܩܪܶܒ, same as ܐܰܟܬܶܒ (Table 3).

TABLE 13. Final Guttural (ܥ). perf. 2nd rad. ܰ - impf. 2nd rad. ܰ : the verb ܫܡܥ , No. 38

Form: $P^{c}al$	*Perfect*	*Imperfect*	*Imperative*	*Act. Part.*	*Pass. Part.*
sing. 3 masc.	ܫܡܥ	ܢܫܡܥ	---	ܫܡܥ	ܫܡܝܥ
sing. 3 fem.	ܫܡܥܬ	ܬܫܡܥ	---	ܫܡܥܐ	* ܫܡܝܥܐ
sing. 2 masc.	ܫܡܥܬ	ܬܫܡܥ	ܫܡܥ	---	---
sing. 2 fem.	* ܫܡܥܬܝ	* ܬܫܡܥܝܢ	* ܫܡܥܝ	---	---
sing. 1 com.	ܫܡܥܬ	ܐܫܡܥ	---	---	---
pl. 3 masc.	ܫܡܥܘ	ܢܫܡܥܘܢ	---	ܫܡܥܝܢ	* ܫܡܝܥܝܢ
pl. 3 fem.	ܫܡܥ	* ܢܫܡܥܢ	---	ܫܡܥܢ	* ܫܡܝܥܢ
pl. 2 masc.	ܫܡܥܬܘܢ	ܬܫܡܥܘܢ	ܫܡܥܘ	---	---
pl. 2 fem.	* ܫܡܥܬܝܢ	* ܬܫܡܥܢ	* ܫܡܥܝܢ	---	---
pl. 1 com.	ܫܡܥܢ	ܢܫܡܥ	---	---	---
	Infinitive:	* ܡܫܡܥ			

TABLE 14.

Form: $Ethp^{c}el$	*Perfect*	*Imperfect*	*Imperative*	*Act. Part.*	*Pass. Part.*
sing. 3 masc.	ܐܫܬܡܥ	ܢܫܬܡܥ	---	---	ܡܫܬܡܥ
sing. 3 fem.	ܐܫܬܡܥܬ	* ܬܫܬܡܥ	---	---	ܡܫܬܡܥܐ
sing. 2 masc.	* ܐܫܬܡܥܬ	* ܬܫܬܡܥ	* ܐܫܬܡܝܥ	---	---
sing. 2 fem.	* ܐܫܬܡܥܬܝ	* ܬܫܬܡܥܝܢ	* ܐܫܬܡܝܥܝ	---	---
sing. 1 com.	* ܐܫܬܡܥܬ	* ܐܫܬܡܥ	---	---	---
pl. 3 masc.	ܐܫܬܡܥܘ	ܢܫܬܡܥܘܢ	---	---	ܡܫܬܡܥܝܢ
pl. 3 fem.	* ܐܫܬܡܥ	* ܢܫܬܡܥܢ	---	---	ܡܫܬܡܥܢ
pl. 2 masc.	ܐܫܬܡܥܬܘܢ	ܬܫܬܡܥܘܢ	ܐܫܬܡܝܥܘ	---	---
pl. 2 fem.	* ܐܫܬܡܥܬܝܢ	* ܬܫܬܡܥܢ	* ܐܫܬܡܝܥܝܢ	---	---
pl. 1 com.	* ܐܫܬܡܥܢ	* ܢܫܬܡܥ	---	---	---
	Infinitive:	* ܡܫܬܡܥܘ			

Other Forms. $Af^{c}el$ occurs in ܡܫܡܥ (act. part.), see Table 3.

TABLE 15. Initial ܢ. perf. 2nd rad. ܰ - impf. 2nd rad. ܰ : the verb ܢܣܰܒ , No. 85

Form: P^c^al	Perfect	Imperfect	Imperative	Act. Part.	Pass. Part.
sing. 3 masc.	ܢܣܰܒ	ܢܶܣܰܒ	---	ܢܳܣܶܒ	* ܢܣܺܝܒ
sing. 3 fem.	ܢܶܣܒܰܬ	* ܬܶܣܰܒ	---	ܢܳܣܒܳܐ	* ܢܣܺܝܒܳܐ
sing. 2 masc.	ܢܣܰܒܬ	ܬܶܣܰܒ	ܣܰܒ	---	---
sing. 2 fem.	* ܢܣܰܒܬܝ	* ܬܶܣܒܺܝܢ	* ܣܰܒܝ	---	---
sing. 1 com.	ܢܶܣܒܶܬ	ܐܶܣܰܒ	---	---	---
pl. 3 masc.	ܢܣܰܒܘ	ܢܶܣܒܽܘܢ	---	ܢܳܣܒܺܝܢ	* ܢܣܺܝܒܺܝܢ
pl. 3 fem.	ܢܣܰܒ	* ܢܶܣܒܳܢ	---	* ܢܳܣܒܳܢ	* ܢܣܺܝܒܳܢ
pl. 2 masc.	ܢܣܰܒܬܽܘܢ	ܬܶܣܒܽܘܢ	ܣܰܒܘ	---	---
pl. 2 fem.	* ܢܣܰܒܬܶܝܢ	* ܬܶܣܒܳܢ	* ܣܰܒܶܝܢ	---	---
pl. 1 com.	ܢܣܰܒܢ	ܢܶܣܰܒ	---	---	---
	Infinitive:	* ܡܶܣܰܒ			

Other Forms. Ethp^c^el occurs in ܢܶܬܢܣܶܒ (impf. s. 3 m.) and ܬܶܬܢܣܶܒ (impf. s. 3 f.), see Table 2.

TABLE 16. Initial ܢ. perf. 2nd rad. ܰ - impf. 2nd rad. ܶ : the verb ܢܦܰܠ , No. 121

Form: P^c^al	Perfect	Imperfect	Imperative	Act. Part.	Pass. Part.
sing. 3 masc.	ܢܦܰܠ	ܢܶܦܶܠ	---	ܢܳܦܶܠ	* ܢܦܺܝܠ
sing. 3 fem.	ܢܶܦܠܰܬ	ܬܶܦܶܠ	---	ܢܳܦܠܳܐ	* ܢܦܺܝܠܳܐ
sing. 2 masc.	* ܢܦܰܠܬ	ܬܶܦܶܠ	ܦܶܠ	---	---
sing. 2 fem.	* ܢܦܰܠܬܝ	* ܬܶܦܠܺܝܢ	* ܦܶܠܝ	---	---
sing. 1 com.	ܢܶܦܠܶܬ	* ܐܶܦܶܠ	---	---	---
pl. 3 masc.	ܢܦܰܠܘ	ܢܶܦܠܽܘܢ	---	ܢܳܦܠܺܝܢ	* ܢܦܺܝܠܺܝܢ
pl. 3 fem.	ܢܦܰܠ	* ܢܶܦܠܳܢ	---	* ܢܳܦܠܳܢ	* ܢܦܺܝܠܳܢ
pl. 2 masc.	ܢܦܰܠܬܽܘܢ	ܬܶܦܠܽܘܢ	ܦܶܠܘ	---	---
pl. 2 fem.	* ܢܦܰܠܬܶܝܢ	* ܬܶܦܠܳܢ	* ܦܶܠܶܝܢ	---	---
pl. 1 com.	ܢܦܰܠܢ	ܢܶܦܶܠ	---	---	---
	Infinitive:	* ܡܶܦܰܠ			

TABLE 17. Initial ܢ. perf. 2nd rad. ݁ – impf. 2nd rad. ݂ܘ : the verb ܢܦܩ , No. 49

Form: P‘al	Perfect	Imperfect	Imperative	Act. Part.	Pass. Part.
sing. 3 masc.	ܢܦܰܩ	ܢܶܦܽܘܩ	---	ܢܳܦܶܩ	ܢܦܺܝܩ
sing. 3 fem.	ܢܶܦܩܰܬ݂	ܬܶܦܽܘܩ	---	ܢܳܦܩܳܐ	* ܢܦܺܝܩܳܐ
sing. 2 masc.	ܢܦܰܩܬ݂	ܬܶܦܽܘܩ	ܦܽܘܩ	---	---
sing. 2 fem.	* ܢܦܰܩܬ̱ܝ	ܬܶܦܩܺܝܢ	ܦܽܘܩܝ	---	---
sing. 1 com.	ܢܶܦܩܶܬ݂	ܐܶܦܽܘܩ	---	---	---
pl. 3 masc.	ܢܦܰܩܘ	ܢܶܦܩܽܘܢ	---	ܢܳܦܩܺܝܢ	* ܢܦܺܝܩܺܝܢ
pl. 3 fem.	ܢܦܰܩ	* ܢܶܦܩܳܢ	---	ܢܳܦܩܳܢ	* ܢܦܺܝܩܳܢ
pl. 2 masc.	ܢܦܰܩܬ݁ܘܢ	ܬܶܦܩܽܘܢ	ܦܽܘܩܘ	---	---
pl. 2 fem.	* ܢܦܰܩܬ݁ܶܝܢ	* ܬܶܦܩܳܢ	* ܦܽܘܩܶܝܢ	---	---
pl. 1 com.	ܢܦܰܩܢ	ܢܶܦܽܘܩ	---	---	---
Infinitive:	* ܡܶܦܰܩ				

Other Forms. Ethpa‘‘al occurs in ܐܶܬ݂ܢܰܦܰܩܘ (perf. pl. 3 m.), see Table 12.

TABLE 18.

Form: Af‘el	Perfect	Imperfect	Imperative	Act. Part.	Pass. Part.
sing. 3 masc.	ܐܰܦܶܩ	ܢܰܦܶܩ	---	ܡܰܦܶܩ	* ܡܰܦܰܩ
sing. 3 fem.	ܐܰܦܩܰܬ݂	ܬܰܦܶܩ	---	* ܡܰܦܩܳܐ	* ܡܰܦܩܳܐ
sing. 2 masc.	ܐܰܦܶܩܬ݂	ܬܰܦܶܩ	ܐܰܦܶܩ	---	---
sing. 2 fem.	* ܐܰܦܶܩܬ̱ܝ	* ܬܰܦܩܺܝܢ	* ܐܰܦܶܩܝ	---	---
sing. 1 com.	ܐܰܦܩܶܬ݂	ܐܰܦܶܩ	---	---	---
pl. 3 masc.	ܐܰܦܶܩܘ	ܢܰܦܩܽܘܢ	---	ܡܰܦܩܺܝܢ	* ܡܰܦܩܺܝܢ
pl. 3 fem.	* ܐܰܦܶܩ	ܢܰܦܩܳܢ	---	* ܡܰܦܩܳܢ	* ܡܰܦܩܳܢ
pl. 2 masc.	* ܐܰܦܶܩܬ݁ܘܢ	* ܬܰܦܩܽܘܢ	ܐܰܦܶܩܘ	---	---
pl. 2 fem.	* ܐܰܦܶܩܬ݁ܶܝܢ	* ܬܰܦܩܳܢ	* ܐܰܦܶܩܶܝܢ	---	---
pl. 1 com.	ܐܰܦܶܩܢ	ܢܰܦܶܩ	---	---	---
Infinitive:	* ܡܰܦܳܩܽܘ				

Verbal Paradigms

TABLE 19. Initial ܝ. perf. 2nd rad. ˚ – impf. 2nd rad. oˆ : the verb ܢܫܒ , No. 161

Form: P^cal	Perfect	Imperfect	Imperative	Act. Part.	Pass. Part.
sing. 3 masc.	ܢܫܒ	ܢܫܘܒ	—	ܢܫܒ	* ܢܫܝܒ
sing. 3 fem.	ܢܫܒܐ	ܐܢܫܘܒ	—	ܢܫܒܐ	* ܢܫܝܒܐ
sing. 2 masc.	* ܢܫܒܬ	* ܐܢܫܘܒ	ܢܫܘܒ	—	—
sing. 2 fem.	* ܢܫܒܬܝ	* ܐܢܫܒܝܢ	* ܢܫܘܒܝ	—	—
sing. 1 com.	ܢܫܒܬ	* ܐܢܫܘܒ	—	—	—
pl. 3 masc.	ܢܫܒܘ	ܢܫܒܘܢ	—	ܢܫܒܝܢ	* ܢܫܝܒܝܢ
pl. 3 fem.	* ܢܫܒ	* ܢܫܒܢ	—	* ܢܫܒܢ	* ܢܫܝܒܢ
pl. 2 masc.	ܢܫܒܬܘܢ	* ܐܢܫܒܘܢ	* ܢܫܘܒܘ	—	—
pl. 2 fem.	* ܢܫܒܬܝܢ	* ܐܢܫܒܢ	* ܢܫܘܒܝܢ	—	—
pl. 1 com.	ܢܫܒܢ	ܢܫܘܒ	—	—	—
Infinitive:	* ܡܢܫܒ				

Other Forms. Af^cel = ܐܫܒ", same as ܐܩܡ" (Table 18).

TABLE 20. Double: the verb ܡܚܟ , No. 55

Form: Pa^{cc}el	Perfect	Imperfect	Imperative	Act. Part.	Pass. Part.
sing. 3 masc.	ܡܚܟ	ܢܡܚܟ	—	ܡܡܚܟ	* ܡܡܚܟ
sing. 3 fem.	ܡܚܟܬ	* ܐܡܚܟܐ	—	ܡܡܚܟܐ	ܡܡܚܟܐ
sing. 2 masc.	ܡܚܟܬ	* ܐܡܚܟ	ܡܚܟ	—	—
sing. 2 fem.	* ܡܚܟܬܝ	* ܐܡܚܟܝܢ	* ܡܚܟܝ	—	—
sing. 1 com.	ܡܚܟܬ	ܐܡܚܟ	—	—	—
pl. 3 masc.	ܡܚܟܘ	ܢܡܚܟܘܢ	—	ܡܡܚܟܝܢ	* ܡܡܚܟܝܢ
pl. 3 fem.	* ܡܚܟ	ܢܡܚܟܢ	—	ܡܡܚܟܢ	* ܡܡܚܟܢ
pl. 2 masc.	* ܡܚܟܬܘܢ	* ܐܡܚܟܘܢ	ܡܚܟܘ	—	—
pl. 2 fem.	ܡܚܟܬܝܢ	* ܐܡܚܟܢ	* ܡܚܟܝܢ	—	—
pl. 1 com.	ܡܚܟܢ	ܢܡܚܟ	—	—	—
Infinitive:	* ܡܡܚܟܘ				

TABLE 21.

Form: Ethpaᶜᶜal	Perfect	Imperfect	Imperative	Act. Part.	Pass. Part.
sing. 3 masc.	ܐܶܬܗܰܡܰܟ݂	ܢܶܬܗܰܡܰܟ݂	---	---	ܡܶܬܗܰܡܰܟ݂
sing. 3 fem.	ܐܶܬܗܰܡܟ݂ܰܬ݂	* ܬܶܬܗܰܡܰܟ݂	---	---	ܡܶܬܗܰܡܟ݂ܳܐ
sing. 2 masc.	* ܐܶܬܗܰܡܰܟ݂ܬ	* ܬܶܬܗܰܡܰܟ݂	* ܐܶܬܗܰܡܰܟ݂	---	---
sing. 2 fem.	* ܐܶܬܗܰܡܰܟ݂ܬܝ	* ܬܶܬܗܰܡܟ݂ܝܢ	* ܐܶܬܗܰܡܟ݂ܝ	---	---
sing. 1 com.	* ܐܶܬܗܰܡܟ݂ܶܬ	ܐܶܬܗܰܡܰܟ݂	---	---	---
pl. 3 masc.	* ܐܶܬܗܰܡܰܟ݂ܘ	ܢܶܬܗܰܡܟ݂ܘܢ	---	---	* ܡܶܬܗܰܡܟ݂ܝܢ
pl. 3 fem.	ܐܶܬܗܰܡܰܟ݂	ܢܶܬܗܰܡܟ݂ܳܢ	---	---	ܡܶܬܗܰܡܟ݂ܳܢ
pl. 2 masc.	* ܐܶܬܗܰܡܰܟ݂ܬܘܢ	* ܬܶܬܗܰܡܟ݂ܘܢ	* ܐܶܬܗܰܡܟ݂ܘ	---	---
pl. 2 fem.	* ܐܶܬܗܰܡܰܟ݂ܬܶܝܢ	* ܬܶܬܗܰܡܟ݂ܳܢ	* ܐܶܬܗܰܡܟ݂ܶܝܢ	---	---
pl. 1 com.	* ܐܶܬܗܰܡܰܟ݂ܢ	ܢܶܬܗܰܡܰܟ݂	---	---	---
Infinitive:	* ܡܶܬܗܰܡܳܟ݂ܘ				

TABLE 22. Double: the verb ܥܰܠ , No. 73

Form: Pᶜal	Perfect	Imperfect	Imperative	Act. Part.	Pass. Part.
sing. 3 masc.	ܥܰܠ	ܢܶܥܘܠ	---	ܥܳܐܶܠ	* ܥܺܝܠ
sing. 3 fem.	ܥܶܠܰܬ݂	* ܬܶܥܘܠ	---	ܥܳܐܠܳܐ	* ܥܺܝܠܳܐ
sing. 2 masc.	ܥܶܠܬ	ܬܶܥܘܠ	* ܥܽܘܠ	---	---
sing. 2 fem.	* ܥܶܠܬܝ	ܬܶܥܠܝܢ	ܥܽܘܠܝ	---	---
sing. 1 com.	ܥܶܠܶܬ	ܐܶܥܘܠ	---	---	---
pl. 3 masc.	ܥܰܠܘ	ܢܶܥܠܘܢ	---	ܥܳܐܠܝܢ	ܥܺܝܠܝܢ
pl. 3 fem.	ܥܰܠܶܝܢ	* ܬܶܥܠܳܢ	---	ܥܳܐܠܳܢ	* ܥܺܝܠܳܢ
pl. 2 masc.	ܥܰܠܬܘܢ	ܬܶܥܠܘܢ	ܥܽܘܠܘ	---	---
pl. 2 fem.	* ܥܰܠܬܶܝܢ	* ܬܶܥܠܳܢ	* ܥܽܘܠܶܝܢ	---	---
pl. 1 com.	ܥܰܠܢ	ܢܶܥܘܠ	---	---	---
Infinitive:	* ܡܶܥܰܠ				

Other Forms. Ethpaᶜᶜal occurs in ܐܶܬܬܥܶܠ (perf. s. 3 m.), see Table 21.

TABLE 23.

Form: Af^{c}el	Perfect	Imperfect	Imperative	Act. Part.	Pass. Part.
sing. 3 masc.	ܐܥܠ	* ܢܥܠ	—	ܡܥܠ	* ܡܥܠ
sing. 3 fem.	ܐܥܠܬ	* ܬܥܠ	—	* ܡܥܠܐ	* ܡܥܠܐ
sing. 2 masc.	* ܐܥܠܬ	* ܬܥܠ	ܐܥܠ	---	---
sing. 2 fem.	* ܐܥܠܬܝ	* ܬܥܠܝܢ	* ܐܥܠܝ	---	---
sing. 1 com.	* ܐܥܠܬ	* ܐܥܠ	---	---	---
pl. 3 masc.	ܐܥܠܘ	ܢܥܠܘܢ	—	ܡܥܠܝܢ	* ܡܥܠܝܢ
pl. 3 fem.	* ܐܥܠ	* ܢܥܠ̈ܢ	---	* ܡܥܠ̈ܢ	* ܡܥܠ̈ܢ
pl. 2 masc.	* ܐܥܠܬܘܢ	* ܬܥܠܘܢ	* ܐܥܠܘ	---	—
pl. 2 fem.	* ܐܥܠܬܝܢ	* ܬܥܠ̈ܢ	* ܐܥܠ̈ܝܢ	---	---
pl. 1 com.	ܐܥܠܢ	* ܢܥܠ	---	---	---
	Infinitive:	* ܡܥܠܘ			

TABLE 24. **Initial** ܐ. perf. 2nd rad. ܰ - impf. 2nd rad. ܰ : the verb ܐܡܪ , No. 5

Form: P^{c}al	Perfect	Imperfect	Imperative	Act. Part.	Pass. Part.
sing. 3 masc.	ܐܡܪ	ܢܐܡܪ	—	ܐܡܪ	ܐܡܝܪ
sing. 3 fem.	ܐܡܪܬ	ܬܐܡܪ	—	ܐܡܪܐ	ܐܡܝܪܐ
sing. 2 masc.	ܐܡܪܬ	ܬܐܡܪ	ܐܡܪ	---	---
sing. 2 fem.	ܐܡܪܬܝ	* ܬܐܡܪܝܢ	ܐܡܪܝ	---	---
sing. 1 com.	ܐܡܪܬ	ܐܡܪ	---	---	---
pl. 3 masc.	ܐܡܪܘ	ܢܐܡܪܘܢ	---	ܐܡܪܝܢ	* ܐܡܝܪܝܢ
pl. 3 fem.	ܐܡܪ̈ܝܢ	ܢܐܡܪ̈ܢ	—	ܐܡܪ̈ܢ	* ܐܡܝܪ̈ܢ
pl. 2 masc.	ܐܡܪܬܘܢ	ܬܐܡܪܘܢ	ܐܡܪܘ	---	—
pl. 2 fem.	* ܐܡܪ̈ܬܝܢ	* ܬܐܡܪ̈ܢ	ܐܡܪ̈ܝܢ	---	---
pl. 1 com.	ܐܡܪܢ	ܢܐܡܪ	---	---	---
	Infinitive:	* ܡܐܡܪ			

Other Forms. Ethp^{c}el occurs in ܐܬܐܡܪ (perf. s. 3 m.), ܐܬܐܡܪ̈ (perf. pl. 3 f.), ܬܬܐܡܪ (impf. s. 3 f.), ܡܬܐܡܪ (pass. part. s. m.), and ܡܬܐܡܪܐ (pass. part. s. f.).

TABLE 25. **Initial ܐ.** perf. 2nd rad. ܰ - impf. 2nd rad. ܘܼ : the verb ܐܟܠ, No. 106

Form: P^c^al	Perfect	Imperfect	Imperative	Act. Part.	Pass. Part.
sing. 3 masc.	ܐܟܠ	ܢܐܟܘܠ	—	ܐܟܠ	ܐܟܝܠ *
sing. 3 fem.	ܐܟܠܬ	ܬܐܟܘܠ	—	ܐܟܠܐ	ܐܟܝܠܐ *
sing. 2 masc.	ܐܟܠܬ *	ܬܐܟܘܠ	ܐܟܘܠ	—	—
sing. 2 fem.	ܐܟܠܬܝ *	ܬܐܟܠܝܢ *	ܐܟܘܠܝ	—	—
sing. 1 com.	ܐܟܠܬ	ܐܟܘܠ	—	—	—
pl. 3 masc.	ܐܟܠܘ	ܢܐܟܠܘܢ	—	ܐܟܠܝܢ	ܐܟܝܠܝܢ *
pl. 3 fem.	ܐܟܠ *	ܢܐܟܠܢ *	—	ܐܟܠܢ	ܐܟܝܠܢ *
pl. 2 masc.	ܐܟܠܬܘܢ	ܬܐܟܠܘܢ	ܐܟܘܠܘ	—	—
pl. 2 fem.	ܐܟܠܬܝܢ *	ܬܐܟܠܢ *	ܐܟܘܠܝܢ *	—	—
pl. 1 com.	ܐܟܠܢ	ܢܐܟܘܠ	—	—	—
Infinitive:	ܡܐܟܠ *				

Other Forms. Ethp^c^el occurs in ܐܬܐܟܠܘ (perf. pl. 3 m.). Af^c^el occurs in ܐܘܟܠ (impf. s. 1 c., and impt. s. m.), see Table 3.

TABLE 26. **Middle ܐ** : the verb ܫܐܠ, No. 79

Form: P^c^al	Perfect	Imperfect	Imperative	Act. Part.	Pass. Part.
sing. 3 masc.	ܫܐܠ	ܢܫܐܠ	—	ܫܐܠ	ܫܐܝܠ *
sing. 3 fem.	ܫܐܠܬ	ܬܫܐܠ	—	ܫܐܠܐ	ܫܐܝܠܐ *
sing. 2 masc.	ܫܐܠܬ	ܬܫܐܠ	ܫܐܠ	—	—
sing. 2 fem.	ܫܐܠܬܝ *	ܬܫܐܠܝܢ	ܫܐܠܝ	—	—
sing. 1 com.	ܫܐܠܬ *	ܐܫܐܠ *	—	—	—
pl. 3 masc.	ܫܐܠܘ	ܢܫܐܠܘܢ	—	ܫܐܠܝܢ	ܫܐܝܠܝܢ *
pl. 3 fem.	ܫܐܠ *	ܢܫܐܠܢ *	—	ܫܐܠܢ	ܫܐܝܠܢ *
pl. 2 masc.	ܫܐܠܬܘܢ	ܬܫܐܠܘܢ	ܫܐܠܘ	—	—
pl. 2 fem.	ܫܐܠܬܝܢ *	ܬܫܐܠܢ *	ܫܐܠܝܢ *	—	—
pl. 1 com.	ܫܐܠܢ	ܢܫܐܠ	—	—	—
Infinitive:	ܡܫܐܠ *				

TABLE 27.

Form: Ethp^{c}el	Perfect	Imperfect	Imperative	Act. Part.	Pass. Part.
sing. 3 masc.	* ܐܫܬܐܠ	* ܢܫܬܐܠ	—	—	* ܡܫܬܐܠ
sing. 3 fem.	* ܐܫܬܐܠܬ	* ܬܫܬܐܠ	—	—	* ܡܫܬܐܠܐ
sing. 2 masc.	* ܐܫܬܐܠܬ	* ܬܫܬܐܠ	ܐܫܬܐܠ	—	—
sing. 2 fem.	* ܐܫܬܐܠܬܝ	* ܬܫܬܐܠܝܢ	* ܐܫܬܐܠܝ	—	—
sing. 1 com.	ܐܫܬܐܠܬ	* ܐܫܬܐܠ	—	—	—
pl. 3 masc.	ܐܫܬܐܠܘ	* ܢܫܬܐܠܘܢ	—	—	* ܡܫܬܐܠܝܢ
pl. 3 fem.	* ܐܫܬܐܠ	* ܢܫܬܐܠܢ	—	—	* ܡܫܬܐܠܢ
pl. 2 masc.	* ܐܫܬܐܠܬܘܢ	ܬܫܬܐܠܘܢ	* ܐܫܬܐܠܘ	—	—
pl. 2 fem.	* ܐܫܬܐܠܬܝܢ	* ܬܫܬܐܠܢ	* ܐܫܬܐܠܝܢ	—	—
pl. 1 com.	* ܐܫܬܐܠܢ	ܢܫܬܐܠ	—	—	—
	Infinitive:	* ܡܫܬܐܠܘ			

TABLE 28.

Form: Pa^{cc}el	Perfect	Imperfect	Imperative	Act. Part.	Pass. Part.
sing. 3 masc.	ܫܐܠ	* ܢܫܐܠ	—	ܡܫܐܠ	* ܡܫܐܠ
sing. 3 fem.	* ܫܐܠܬ	* ܬܫܐܠ	—	* ܡܫܐܠܐ	* ܡܫܐܠܐ
sing. 2 masc.	* ܫܐܠܬ	* ܬܫܐܠ	ܫܐܠ	—	—
sing. 2 fem.	* ܫܐܠܬܝ	* ܬܫܐܠܝܢ	* ܫܐܠܝ	—	—
sing. 1 com.	* ܫܐܠܬ	* ܐܫܐܠ	—	—	—
pl. 3 masc.	ܫܐܠܘ	* ܢܫܐܠܘܢ	—	ܡܫܐܠܝܢ	* ܡܫܐܠܝܢ
pl. 3 fem.	* ܫܐܠ	ܢܫܐܠܢ	—	* ܡܫܐܠܢ	* ܡܫܐܠܢ
pl. 2 masc.	* ܫܐܠܬܘܢ	* ܬܫܐܠܘܢ	ܫܐܠܘ	—	—
pl. 2 fem.	* ܫܐܠܬܝܢ	* ܬܫܐܠܢ	* ܫܐܠܝܢ	—	—
pl. 1 com.	* ܫܐܠܢ	* ܢܫܐܠ	—	—	—
	Infinitive:	* ܡܫܐܠܘ			

Other Forms. Ethpa^{cc}al occurs in ܐܫܬܐܠ (perf. s. 3 m.) and ܢܫܬܐܠ (impf. s. 3 m.). Af^{c}el occurs in ܐܫܐܠ (impt. s. m.).

Verbal Paradigms

TABLE 29. Final ܐ : the verb ܣܢܐ , No. 28

Form: P^cal	Perfect	Imperfect	Imperative	Act. Part.	Pass. Part.
sing. 3 masc.	ܣܢܐ	ܢܣܢܐ	---	ܣܳܢܶܐ	ܣܢܶܐ
sing. 3 fem.	ܣܢܳܬ݀	ܬܶܣܢܶܐ *	---	ܣܳܢܝܳܐ *	ܣܢܝܳܐ *
sing. 2 masc.	ܣܢܰܝܬ	ܬܶܣܢܶܐ	ܣܢܺܝ	---	---
sing. 2 fem.	ܣܢܰܝܬܝ *	ܬܶܣܢܶܝܢ	ܣܢܳܝ *	---	---
sing. 1 com.	ܣܢܺܝܬ	ܐܶܣܢܶܐ	---	---	---
pl. 3 masc.	ܣܢܰܘ	ܢܶܣܢܘܢ	---	ܣܳܢܶܝܢ	ܣܢܶܝܢ *
pl. 3 fem.	ܣܢܳܝ	ܢܶܣܢܝܳܢ	---	ܣܳܢܝܳܢ	ܣܢܝܳܢ *
pl. 2 masc.	ܣܢܰܝܬܘܢ	ܬܶܣܢܘܢ	ܣܢܰܘ	---	---
pl. 2 fem.	ܣܢܰܝܬܶܝܢ *	ܬܶܣܢܝܳܢ *	ܣܢܳܝ	---	---
pl. 1 com.	ܣܢܰܝܢ	ܢܶܣܢܶܐ	---	---	---
Infinitive:	ܡܶܣܢܳܐ *				

TABLE 30.

Form: Ethp^cel	Perfect	Imperfect	Imperative	Act. Part.	Pass. Part.
sing. 3 masc.	ܐܶܬܣܢܺܝ	ܢܶܬܣܢܶܐ	---	---	ܡܶܬܣܢܶܐ
sing. 3 fem.	ܐܶܬܣܰܢܝܰܬ	ܬܶܬܣܢܶܐ	---	---	ܡܶܬܣܰܢܝܳܐ
sing. 2 masc.	ܐܶܬܣܢܺܝܬ *	ܬܶܬܣܢܶܐ	ܐܶܬܣܢܺܝ *	---	---
sing. 2 fem.	ܐܶܬܣܢܺܝܬܝ *	ܬܶܬܣܢܶܝܢ *	ܐܶܬܣܢܳܝ *	---	---
sing. 1 com.	ܐܶܬܣܢܺܝܬ	ܐܶܬܣܢܶܐ *	---	---	---
pl. 3 masc.	ܐܶܬܣܢܺܝܘ	ܢܶܬܣܢܘܢ	---	---	ܡܶܬܣܰܢܝܳܢ
pl. 3 fem.	ܐܶܬܣܢܺܝ	ܢܶܬܣܰܢܝܳܢ	---	---	ܡܶܬܣܰܢܝܳܢ
pl. 2 masc.	ܐܶܬܣܢܺܝܬܘܢ *	ܬܶܬܣܢܘܢ	ܐܶܬܣܢܰܘ	---	---
pl. 2 fem.	ܐܶܬܣܢܺܝܬܶܝܢ *	ܬܶܬܣܰܢܝܳܢ *	ܐܶܬܣܢܰܝܶܝܢ *	---	---
pl. 1 com.	ܐܶܬܣܢܺܝܢ *	ܢܶܬܣܢܶܐ *	---	---	---
Infinitive:	ܡܶܬܣܰܢܳܝܘ *				

TABLE 31. Initial and Final ܐ : the verb ܐܬܳܐ , No. 18

Form: P^{c}al	*Perfect*	*Imperfect*	*Imperative*	*Act. Part.*	*Pass. Part.*
sing. 3 masc.	ܐܬܳܐ	ܢܺܐܬܶܐ	---	ܐܳܬܶܐ	ܐܬܺܝ *
sing. 3 fem.	ܐܬܳܬ	ܬܺܐܬܶܐ	---	ܐܳܬܝܳܐ	ܐܬܝܳܐ *
sing. 2 masc.	ܐܬܰܝܬ	ܬܺܐܬܶܐ	ܬܳܐ	---	---
sing. 2 fem.	ܐܬܰܝܬܝ *	ܬܺܐܬܶܝܢ *	ܬܳܝ	---	---
sing. 1 com.	ܐܬܺܝܬ	ܐܺܬܶܐ	---	---	---
pl. 3 masc.	ܐܬܰܘ	ܢܺܐܬܽܘܢ	---	ܐܳܬܶܝܢ	ܐܬܶܝܢ
pl. 3 fem.	ܐܬܰܝ̈	ܢܺܐܬܝܳܢ	---	ܐܳܬܝ̈ܳܢ	ܐܬܝ̈ܳܢ *
pl. 2 masc.	ܐܬܰܝܬܽܘܢ	ܬܺܐܬܽܘܢ	ܬܰܘ	---	---
pl. 2 fem.	ܐܬܰܝܬܶܝܢ *	ܬܺܐܬܝ̈ܳܢ *	ܬܳܝܶܝܢ	---	---
pl. 1 com.	ܐܬܶܝܢ	ܢܺܐܬܶܐ	---	---	---
	Infinitive:	ܡܶܐܬܳܐ *			

Other Forms. Pa^{cc}el occurs in ܐܰܬܺܝ (perf. s. 3 m.).

TABLE 32.

Form: Af^{c}el	*Perfect*	*Imperfect*	*Imperative*	*Act. Part.*	*Pass. Part.*
sing. 3 masc.	ܐܰܝܬܺܝ	ܢܰܝܬܶܐ	---	ܡܰܝܬܶܐ	ܡܰܝܬܰܐ *
sing. 3 fem.	ܐܰܝܬܝܰܬ *	ܬܰܝܬܶܐ	---	ܡܰܝܬܝܳܐ	ܡܰܝܬܝܳܐ *
sing. 2 masc.	ܐܰܝܬܺܝܬ *	ܬܰܝܬܶܐ *	ܐܰܝܬܳܐ	---	---
sing. 2 fem.	ܐܰܝܬܺܝܬܝ *	ܬܰܝܬܶܝܢ *	ܐܰܝܬܳܝ *	---	---
sing. 1 com.	ܐܰܝܬܺܝܬ	ܐܰܝܬܶܐ	---	---	---
pl. 3 masc.	ܐܰܝܬܺܝܘ	ܢܰܝܬܽܘܢ	---	ܡܰܝܬܶܝܢ	ܡܰܝܬܶܝܢ *
pl. 3 fem.	ܐܰܝܬܺܝ̈	ܢܰܝܬܝ̈ܳܢ *	---	ܡܰܝܬܝ̈ܳܢ *	ܡܰܝܬܝ̈ܳܢ *
pl. 2 masc.	ܐܰܝܬܺܝܬܽܘܢ	ܬܰܝܬܽܘܢ	ܐܰܝܬܰܘ	---	---
pl. 2 fem.	ܐܰܝܬܺܝܬܶܝܢ *	ܬܰܝܬܝ̈ܳܢ *	ܐܰܝܬܳܝܶܝܢ *	---	---
pl. 1 com.	ܐܰܝܬܺܝܢ *	ܢܰܝܬܶܐ *	---	---	---
	Infinitive:	ܡܰܝܬܳܝܽܘ *			

Verbal Paradigms

TABLE 33. Initial ܝ and Final Guttural (ܥ). perf. 2nd rad. ˊ – impf. 2nd rad. ˊ : the verb ܝܕܥ, No. 32

Form: Pᶜal	Perfect	Imperfect	Imperative	Act. Part.	Pass. Part.
sing. 3 masc.	ܝܕܥ	ܢܕܥ	---	ܝܕܥ	ܝܕܝܥ
sing. 3 fem.	ܝܕܥܬ	ܬܕܥ	---	ܝܕܥܐ	ܝܕܝܥܐ
sing. 2 masc.	ܝܕܥܬ *	ܬܕܥ	ܕܥ	---	---
sing. 2 fem.	ܝܕܥܬܝ *	ܬܕܥܝܢ *	ܕܥܝ *	---	---
sing. 1 com.	ܝܕܥܬ	ܐܕܥ	---	---	---
pl. 3 masc.	ܝܕܥܘ	ܢܕܥܘܢ	---	ܝܕܥܝܢ	ܝܕܝܥܝܢ
pl. 3 fem.	ܝܕܥ *	ܢܕܥܢ *	---	ܝܕܥܢ	ܝܕܝܥܢ *
pl. 2 masc.	ܝܕܥܬܘܢ	ܬܕܥܘܢ	ܕܥܘ	---	---
pl. 2 fem.	ܝܕܥܬܝܢ *	ܬܕܥܢ *	ܕܥܝܢ *	---	---
pl. 1 com.	ܝܕܥܢ	ܢܕܥ	---	---	---
Infinitive:	ܡܕܥ *				

TABLE 34.

Form: Ethpᶜel	Perfect	Imperfect	Imperative	Act. Part.	Pass. Part.
sing. 3 masc.	ܐܬܝܕܥ	ܢܬܝܕܥ	---	---	ܡܬܝܕܥ
sing. 3 fem.	ܐܬܝܕܥܬ	ܬܬܝܕܥ	---	---	ܡܬܝܕܥܐ
sing. 2 masc.	ܐܬܝܕܥܬ *	ܬܬܝܕܥ *	ܐܬܝܕܥ *	---	---
sing. 2 fem.	ܐܬܝܕܥܬܝ *	ܬܬܝܕܥܝܢ *	ܐܬܝܕܥܝ *	---	---
sing. 1 com.	ܐܬܝܕܥܬ	ܐܬܝܕܥ *	---	---	---
pl. 3 masc.	ܐܬܝܕܥܘ *	ܢܬܝܕܥܘܢ	---	---	ܡܬܝܕܥܝܢ *
pl. 3 fem.	ܐܬܝܕܥ *	ܢܬܝܕܥܢ	---	---	ܡܬܝܕܥܢ
pl. 2 masc.	ܐܬܝܕܥܬܘܢ	ܬܬܝܕܥܘܢ *	ܐܬܝܕܥܘ *	---	---
pl. 2 fem.	ܐܬܝܕܥܬܝܢ *	ܬܬܝܕܥܢ *	ܐܬܝܕܥܝܢ *	---	---
pl. 1 com.	ܐܬܝܕܥܢ *	ܢܬܝܕܥ *	---	---	---
Infinitive:	ܡܬܝܕܥܘ *				

Verbal Paradigms

TABLE 35.

Form: Af‑el	Perfect	Imperfect	Imperative	Act. Part.	Pass. Part.
sing. 3 masc.	ܐܘܙܒ	ܢܘܙܒ	---	ܡܘܙܒ	* ܡܘܙܒ
sing. 3 fem.	* ܐܘܙܒܬ	* ܐܘܙܒ	---	ܡܘܙܒܐ	* ܡܘܙܒܐ
sing. 2 masc.	* ܐܘܙܒܬ	* ܐܘܙܒ	* ܐܘܙܒ	---	---
sing. 2 fem.	* ܐܘܙܒܬܝ	* ܐܘܙܒܝܢ	* ܐܘܙܒܝ	---	---
sing. 1 com.	ܐܘܙܒܬ	ܐܘܙܒ	---	---	---
pl. 3 masc.	ܐܘܙܒܘ	ܢܘܙܒܘܢ	---	* ܡܘܙܒܝܢ	* ܡܘܙܒܝܢ
pl. 3 fem.	* ܐܘܙܒ	* ܢܘܙܒܢ	---	* ܡܘܙܒܢ	* ܡܘܙܒܢ
pl. 2 masc.	* ܐܘܙܒܬܘܢ	* ܐܘܙܒܘܢ	* ܐܘܙܒܘ	---	---
pl. 2 fem.	* ܐܘܙܒܬܝܢ	* ܐܘܙܒܢ	* ܐܘܙܒܝܢ	---	---
pl. 1 com.	* ܐܘܙܒܢ	* ܢܘܙܒ	---	---	---

Infinitive: * ܡܘܙܒܘ

Other Forms. Šaf‑el occurs in ܫܘܙܒ (perf. s. 3 m.).

TABLE 36.

Form: Eštaf‑al	Perfect	Imperfect	Imperative	Act. Part.	Pass. Part.
sing. 3 masc.	ܐܫܬܘܙܒ	* ܢܫܬܘܙܒ	---	---	* ܡܫܬܘܙܒ
sing. 3 fem.	ܐܫܬܘܙܒܬ	* ܐܫܬܘܙܒ	---	---	* ܡܫܬܘܙܒܐ
sing. 2 masc.	* ܐܫܬܘܙܒܬ	* ܐܫܬܘܙܒ	* ܐܫܬܘܙܒ	---	---
sing. 2 fem.	* ܐܫܬܘܙܒܬܝ	* ܐܫܬܘܙܒܝܢ	* ܐܫܬܘܙܒܝ	---	---
sing. 1 com.	* ܐܫܬܘܙܒܬ	ܐܫܬܘܙܒ	---	---	---
pl. 3 masc.	ܐܫܬܘܙܒܘ	ܢܫܬܘܙܒܘܢ	---	---	* ܡܫܬܘܙܒܝܢ
pl. 3 fem.	ܐܫܬܘܙܒ	* ܢܫܬܘܙܒܢ	---	---	* ܡܫܬܘܙܒܢ
pl. 2 masc.	* ܐܫܬܘܙܒܬܘܢ	* ܐܫܬܘܙܒܘܢ	* ܐܫܬܘܙܒܘ	---	---
pl. 2 fem.	* ܐܫܬܘܙܒܬܝܢ	* ܐܫܬܘܙܒܢ	* ܐܫܬܘܙܒܝܢ	---	---
pl. 1 com.	* ܐܫܬܘܙܒܢ	* ܢܫܬܘܙܒ	---	---	---

Infinitive: * ܡܫܬܘܙܒܘ

TABLE 37. Initial ܝ . perf. 2nd rad. ܰ - impf. 2nd rad. ܳ : the verb ܢܟܰܘ , No. 129

Form: Pᶜal	Perfect	Imperfect	Imperative	Act. Part.	Pass. Part.
sing. 3 masc.	ܢܟܰܘ	ܢܺܐܟܰܘ	—	ܢܳܟܶܘ	* ܢܟܺܘ
sing. 3 fem.	* ܢܶܟܰܬ݂	* ܬܺܐܟܰܘ	—	ܢܳܟܝܳܐ	* ܢܟܺܝܬܳܐ
sing. 2 masc.	ܢܟܰܬ݂	ܬܺܐܟܰܘ	* ܢܟܺܘ	—	—
sing. 2 fem.	* ܢܟܰܬܝ	* ܬܺܐܟܝܢ	* ܢܟܰܝ	—	—
sing. 1 com.	ܢܟܺܬ݂	ܐܟܰܘ	—	—	—
pl. 3 masc.	* ܢܟܰܘ	ܢܺܐܟܘܢ	—	* ܢܟܺܝܢ	* ܢܟܺܝܢ
pl. 3 fem.	* ܢܟܰܝ	ܢܺܐܟܢ	—	ܢܟܳܢ	* ܢܟܺܢ
pl. 2 masc.	ܢܟܰܬܘܢ	ܬܺܐܟܘܢ	ܢܟܰܘ	—	—
pl. 2 fem.	* ܢܟܰܬܝܢ	* ܬܺܐܟܢ	* ܢܟܰܝܢ	—	—
pl. 1 com.	ܢܟܰܢ	ܢܺܐܟܰܘ	—	—	—
Infinitive:	* ܡܟܰܘ				

TABLE 38.

Form: Paᶜᶜel	Perfect	Imperfect	Imperative	Act. Part.	Pass. Part.
sing. 3 masc.	ܢܰܟܺܘ	ܢܰܟܶܘ	—	ܡܢܰܟܶܘ	* ܡܢܰܟܰܘ
sing. 3 fem.	* ܢܰܟܝܰܬ݂	* ܬܢܰܟܶܘ	—	ܡܢܰܟܝܳܐ	ܡܢܰܟܝܳܐ
sing. 2 masc.	ܢܰܟܝܬ݂	* ܬܢܰܟܶܘ	* ܢܰܟܶܘ	—	—
sing. 2 fem.	* ܢܰܟܝܬܝ	ܬܢܰܟܝܢ	* ܢܰܟܰܝ	—	—
sing. 1 com.	ܢܰܟܝܬ݂	ܐܢܰܟܶܘ	—	—	—
pl. 3 masc.	ܢܰܟܝܘ	ܢܢܰܟܘܢ	—	ܡܢܰܟܝܢ	* ܡܢܰܟܝܢ
pl. 3 fem.	* ܢܰܟܝ	ܢܢܰܟܢ	—	ܡܢܰܟܳܢ	* ܡܢܰܟܰܢ
pl. 2 masc.	* ܢܰܟܝܬܘܢ	ܬܢܰܟܘܢ	ܢܰܟܰܘ	—	—
pl. 2 fem.	* ܢܰܟܝܬܝܢ	* ܬܢܰܟܢ	* ܢܰܟܰܝܢ	—	—
pl. 1 com.	* ܢܰܟܝܢ	* ܢܢܰܟܶܘ	—	—	—
Infinitive:	* ܡܢܰܟܳܘܽ				

Other Forms. Ethpaᶜᶜal occurs in ܡܬܢܰܟܝܢ (pass. part. pl. m.).

Verbal Paradigms

TABLE 39. Initial ܝ . perf. 2nd rad. ܲ - impf. 2nd rad. ܲ : the verb ܝܺܠܶܕ݂ , No. 126

Form: Pᶜal	Perfect	Imperfect	Imperative	Act. Part.	Pass. Part.
sing. 3 masc.	ܝܺܠܶܕ݂	ܢܺܐܠܰܕ݂	---	ܝܳܠܶܕ݂	*ܝܺܠܺܝܕ݂
sing. 3 fem.	ܝܶܠܕ݂ܰܬ݂	*ܬܺܐܠܰܕ݂	---	ܝܳܠܕ݂ܳܐ	*ܝܺܠܺܝܕ݂ܳܐ
sing. 2 masc.	*ܝܺܠܶܕ݂ܬ݂	*ܬܺܐܠܰܕ݂	ܝܺܠܰܕ݂	---	---
sing. 2 fem.	*ܝܺܠܶܕ݂ܬ݁ܝ	*ܬܺܐܠܕ݂ܺܝܢ	*ܝܺܠܰܕ݂ܝ	---	---
sing. 1 com.	ܝܺܠܶܕ݂ܶܬ݂	*ܐܺܠܰܕ݂	---	---	---
pl. 3 masc.	ܝܺܠܶܕ݂ܘ	ܢܺܐܠܕ݂ܽܘܢ	---	ܝܳܠܕ݂ܺܝܢ	*ܝܺܠܺܝܕ݂ܺܝܢ
pl. 3 fem.	*ܝܺܠܶܕ݂	*ܬܺܐܠܕ݂ܳܢ	---	ܝܳܠܕ݂ܳܢ	*ܝܺܠܺܝܕ݂ܳܢ
pl. 2 masc.	ܝܺܠܶܕ݂ܬ݁ܽܘܢ	ܬܺܐܠܕ݂ܽܘܢ	ܝܺܠܰܕ݂ܘ	---	---
pl. 2 fem.	*ܝܺܠܶܕ݂ܬ݁ܶܝܢ	*ܬܺܐܠܕ݂ܳܢ	*ܝܺܠܰܕ݂ܶܝܢ	---	---
pl. 1 com.	ܝܺܠܶܕ݂ܢ	ܢܺܐܠܰܕ݂	---	---	---
Infinitive:	*ܡܺܐܠܰܕ݂				

Other Forms. Afᶜel = ܐܰܘܠܶܕ݂ , same as ܐܰܘܕ݂ܺܝ with ܲ on the second radical instead of ܻ (Table 35).

TABLE 40. Middle ܝ : the verb ܣܳܐܶܢ , No. 117

Form: Pᶜal	Perfect	Imperfect	Imperative	Act. Part.	Pass. Part.
sing. 3 masc.	ܣܳܐܶܢ	ܢܣܺܝܢ	---	ܣܳܐܶܢ	*
sing. 3 fem.	ܣܳܢܰܬ݂	ܬܣܺܝܢ	---	ܣܳܝܢܳܐ	*
sing. 2 masc.	*ܣܳܢܬ݂	ܬܣܺܝܢ	*ܣܺܝܢ	---	---
sing. 2 fem.	*ܣܳܢܬ݁ܝ	*ܬܣܺܝܢܺܝܢ	*ܣܺܝܢܝ	---	---
sing. 1 com.	ܣܳܢܶܬ݂	ܐܣܺܝܢ	---	---	---
pl. 3 masc.	ܣܳܢܘ	ܢܣܺܝܢܽܘܢ	---	ܣܳܝܢܺܝܢ	*
pl. 3 fem.	ܣܳܢ	*ܬܣܺܝܢܳܢ	---	*ܣܳܝܢܳܢ	*
pl. 2 masc.	ܣܳܢܬ݁ܽܘܢ	ܬܣܺܝܢܽܘܢ	ܣܺܝܢܘ	---	---
pl. 2 fem.	*ܣܳܢܬ݁ܶܝܢ	*ܬܣܺܝܢܳܢ	*ܣܺܝܢܶܝܢ	---	---
pl. 1 com.	ܣܳܢܢ	ܢܣܺܝܢ	---	---	---
Infinitive:	*ܡܣܳܢ				

Note. In late Western Syriac, the impf. forms are ܢܳܐܣܶܢ , ܐܳܣܶܢ , etc.; inf. ܡܣܳܐܣ .

Verbal Paradigms

TABLE 41.

Form: Af‏ⁿel	Perfect	Imperfect	Imperative	Act. Part.	Pass. Part.
sing. 3 masc.	ܐܰܫܠܺܝ	ܢܰܫܠܶܐ	---	ܡܰܫܠܶܐ	* ܡܰܫܠܰܝ
sing. 3 fem.	* ܐܰܫܠܝܰܬ݀	ܬܰܫܠܶܐ	---	ܡܰܫܠܝܳܐ	* ܡܰܫܠܰܝܳܐ
sing. 2 masc.	* ܐܰܫܠܺܝܬ	ܬܰܫܠܶܐ	ܐܰܫܠܳܐ	---	---
sing. 2 fem.	* ܐܰܫܠܺܝܬܝ	ܬܰܫܠܶܝܢ	* ܐܰܫܠܳܝ	---	---
sing. 1 com.	* ܐܰܫܠܺܝܬ	ܐܰܫܠܶܐ	---	---	---
pl. 3 masc.	ܐܰܫܠܺܝܘ	* ܢܰܫܠܽܘܢ	---	* ܡܰܫܠܶܝܢ	* ܡܰܫܠܰܝܳܐ
pl. 3 fem.	* ܐܰܫܠܺܝ	* ܬܰܫܠܝܳܢ	---	* ܡܰܫܠܝܳܢ	* ܡܰܫܠܰܝܳܢ
pl. 2 masc.	* ܐܰܫܠܺܝܬܽܘܢ	* ܬܰܫܠܽܘܢ	* ܐܰܫܠܰܘ	---	---
pl. 2 fem.	* ܐܰܫܠܺܝܬܶܝܢ	* ܬܰܫܠܝܳܢ	* ܐܰܫܠܝܶܝܢ	---	---
pl. 1 com.	* ܐܰܫܠܺܝܢ	ܢܰܫܠܶܐ	---	---	---
Infinitive:	* ܡܰܫܠܳܝܽܘ				

Note. In late Western Syriac, the impf. forms are ܢܰܫܠܶܐ , ܐܰܫܠܶܐ , etc.; part. ܡܰܫܠܶܐ , etc.; inf. ܡܰܫܠܳܝܽܘ .

TABLE 42. Middle ܘ : the verb ܩܳܡ , No. 94

Form: P‏ⁿal	Perfect	Imperfect	Imperative	Act. Part.	Pass. Part.
sing. 3 masc.	ܩܳܡ	ܢܩܽܘܡ	---	ܩܳܐܶܡ	ܩܺܝܡ
sing. 3 fem.	* ܩܳܡܰܬ݀	* ܬܩܽܘܡ	---	* ܩܳܝܡܳܐ	ܩܺܝܡܳܐ
sing. 2 masc.	ܩܳܡܬ	ܬܩܽܘܡ	ܩܽܘܡ	---	---
sing. 2 fem.	* ܩܳܡܬܝ	ܬܩܽܘܡܺܝܢ	* ܩܽܘܡܝ	---	---
sing. 1 com.	ܩܳܡܶܬ	ܐܩܽܘܡ	---	---	---
pl. 3 masc.	ܩܳܡܘ	ܢܩܽܘܡܽܘܢ	---	ܩܳܝܡܺܝܢ	ܩܺܝܡܺܝܢ
pl. 3 fem.	* ܩܳܡ	* ܬܩܽܘܡܳܢ	---	* ܩܳܝܡܳܢ	ܩܺܝܡܳܢ
pl. 2 masc.	* ܩܳܡܬܽܘܢ	* ܬܩܽܘܡܽܘܢ	ܩܽܘܡܘ	---	---
pl. 2 fem.	* ܩܳܡܬܶܝܢ	* ܬܩܽܘܡܳܢ	* ܩܽܘܡܶܝܢ	---	---
pl. 1 com.	* ܩܳܡܢ	ܢܩܽܘܡ	---	---	---
Infinitive:	* ܡܩܳܡ				

TABLE 43.

Form: Ethpᶜel	Perfect	Imperfect	Imperative	Act. Part.	Pass. Part.
sing. 3 masc.	ܐܶܬ̣ܩܛܶܠ	ܢܶܬ̣ܩܛܶܠ	---	---	ܡܶܬ̣ܩܛܶܠ
sing. 3 fem.	ܐܶܬ̣ܩܰܛܠܰܬ̣ *	ܬܶܬ̣ܩܛܶܠ *	---	---	ܡܶܬ̣ܩܰܛܠܳܐ *
sing. 2 masc.	ܐܶܬ̣ܩܛܶܠܬ̣ *	ܬܶܬ̣ܩܛܶܠ *	ܐܶܬ̣ܩܛܶܠ *	---	---
sing. 2 fem.	ܐܶܬ̣ܩܛܶܠܬ̣ܝ *	ܬܶܬ̣ܩܰܛܠܺܝܢ *	ܐܶܬ̣ܩܰܛܠܺܝ *	---	---
sing. 1 com.	ܐܶܬ̣ܩܛܶܠܬ̣	ܐܶܬ̣ܩܛܶܠ	---	---	---
pl. 3 masc.	ܐܶܬ̣ܩܛܶܠܘ *	ܢܶܬ̣ܩܰܛܠܘܢ	---	---	ܡܶܬ̣ܩܰܛܠܺܝܢ *
pl. 3 fem.	ܐܶܬ̣ܩܛܶܠ	ܢܶܬ̣ܩܰܛܠܳܢ *	---	---	ܡܶܬ̣ܩܰܛܠܳܢ *
pl. 2 masc.	ܐܶܬ̣ܩܛܶܠܬܘܢ *	ܬܶܬ̣ܩܰܛܠܘܢ *	ܐܶܬ̣ܩܰܛܠܘ *	---	---
pl. 2 fem.	ܐܶܬ̣ܩܛܶܠܬܶܝܢ *	ܬܶܬ̣ܩܰܛܠܳܢ *	ܐܶܬ̣ܩܰܛܠܶܝܢ *	---	---
pl. 1 com.	ܐܶܬ̣ܩܛܶܠܢ	ܢܶܬ̣ܩܛܶܠ	---	---	---

Infinitive: ܡܶܬ̣ܩܛܳܠܘ *

Note. The Ethpᶜel forms may have one or two ܬ as in ܐܶܬ̣ܩܛܶܠ or ܐܶܬܬ̣ܩܛܶܠ, etc.

TABLE 44. Middle ܘ : the verb ܩܳܡ, No. 36

Form: Pᶜal	Perfect	Imperfect	Imperative	Act. Part.	Pass. Part.
sing. 3 masc.	ܩܳܡ	ܢܩܘܡ	---	ܩܳܐܶܡ	*
sing. 3 fem.	ܩܳܡܰܬ̣	ܬܩܘܡ	---	ܩܳܝܡܳܐ	*
sing. 2 masc.	ܩܳܡܬ̣	ܬܩܘܡ *	ܩܘܡ	---	---
sing. 2 fem.	ܩܳܡܬ̣ܝ *	ܬܩܘܡܺܝܢ *	ܩܘܡܝ	---	---
sing. 1 com.	ܩܳܡܶܬ̣	ܐܩܘܡ	---	---	---
pl. 3 masc.	ܩܳܡܘ	ܢܩܘܡܘܢ	---	ܩܳܝܡܺܝܢ	*
pl. 3 fem.	ܩܳܡ	ܢܩܘܡܳܢ	---	ܩܳܝܡܳܢ	*
pl. 2 masc.	ܩܳܡܬܘܢ	ܬܩܘܡܘܢ	ܩܘܡܘ	---	---
pl. 2 fem.	ܩܳܡܬܶܝܢ *	ܬܩܘܡܳܢ *	ܩܘܡܶܝܢ *	---	---
pl. 1 com.	ܩܳܡܢ	ܢܩܘܡ *	---	---	---

Infinitive: ܡܩܳܡ *

Other Forms. Paᶜᶜel occurs in ܩܰܝܶܡ (perf. s. 3 m.), ܩܰܝܶܡܘ (perf. pl. 3 m.), ܢܩܰܝܶܡ (impf. s. 3 m.) and ܡܩܰܝܶܡ (act. part. s. m.). Ethpaᶜᶜal occurs in ܬܶܬ̣ܩܰܝܡܘܢ (impf. pl. 2 m.), ܢܶܬ̣ܩܰܝܰܡ (impf. pl. 1 c.), ܐܶܬ̣ܩܰܝܡܘ (impt. pl. m.), ܡܶܬ̣ܩܰܝܰܡ (pass. part. sing m.), and ܡܶܬ̣ܩܰܝܡܺܝܢ (pass. part. pl. m.).

TABLE 45.

Form: Afᶜel	Perfect	Imperfect	Imperative	Act. Part.	Pass. Part.
sing. 3 masc.	ܐܩܝܡ	ܢܩܝܡ	---	ܡܩܝܡ	*
sing. 3 fem.	* ܐܩܝܡܬ	* ܬܩܝܡ	---	* ܡܩܝܡܐ	*
sing. 2 masc.	* ܐܩܝܡܬ	ܬܩܝܡ	* ܐܩܝܡ	---	---
sing. 2 fem.	* ܐܩܝܡܬܝ	* ܬܩܝܡܝܢ	* ܐܩܝܡܝ	---	---
sing. 1 com.	* ܐܩܝܡܬ	* ܐܩܝܡ	---	---	---
pl. 3 masc.	ܐܩܝܡܘ	ܢܩܝܡܘܢ	---	* ܡܩܝܡܝܢ	*
pl. 3 fem.	* ܐܩܝܡ	* ܢܩܝܡܢ	---	ܡܩܝܡܢ	*
pl. 2 masc.	* ܐܩܝܡܬܘܢ	ܬܩܝܡܘܢ	* ܐܩܝܡܘ	---	---
pl. 2 fem.	* ܐܩܝܡܬܝܢ	* ܬܩܝܡܢ	* ܐܩܝܡܝܢ	---	---
pl. 1 com.	* ܐܩܝܡܢ	ܢܩܝܡ	---	---	---
	Infinitive:	* ܡܩܡܘ			

TABLE 46. The verb ܝܗܒ (perfect), ܢܬܠ (imperfect), No. 37

Form: Pᶜal	Perfect	Imperfect	Imperative	Act. Part.	Pass. Part.
sing. 3 masc.	ܝܗܒ	ܢܬܠ	---	ܝܗܒ	ܝܗܝܒ
sing. 3 fem.	ܝܗܒܬ	ܬܬܠ	---	ܝܗܒܐ	ܝܗܝܒܐ
sing. 2 masc.	ܝܗܒܬ	ܬܬܠ	ܗܒ	---	---
sing. 2 fem.	* ܝܗܒܬܝ	* ܬܬܠܝܢ	* ܗܒܝ	---	---
sing. 1 com.	ܝܗܒܬ	ܐܬܠ	---	---	---
pl. 3 masc.	ܝܗܒܘ	ܢܬܠܘܢ	---	ܝܗܒܝܢ	ܝܗܝܒܝܢ
pl. 3 fem.	* ܝܗܒ	ܢܬܠܢ	---	ܝܗܒܢ	* ܝܗܝܒܢ
pl. 2 masc.	ܝܗܒܬܘܢ	ܬܬܠܘܢ	ܗܒܘ	---	---
pl. 2 fem.	* ܝܗܒܬܝܢ	* ܬܬܠܢ	ܗܒܝܢ	---	---
pl. 1 com.	ܝܗܒܢ	ܢܬܠ	---	---	---
	Infinitive:	* ܡܬܠ			

TABLE 47.

Form: Ethp^c^el	Perfect	Imperfect	Imperative	Act. Part.	Pass. Part.
sing. 3 masc.	ܐܬܝܗܒ	ܢܬܝܗܒ	---	---	ܡܬܝܗܒ
sing. 3 fem.	ܐܬܝܗܒܬ	ܬܬܝܗܒ	---	---	ܡܬܝܗܒܐ
sing. 2 masc.	* ܐܬܝܗܒܬ	* ܬܬܝܗܒ	* ܐܬܝܗܒ	---	---
sing. 2 fem.	* ܐܬܝܗܒܬܝ	* ܬܬܝܗܒܝܢ	* ܐܬܝܗܒܝ	---	---
sing. 1 com.	* ܐܬܝܗܒܬ	* ܐܬܝܗܒ	---	---	---
pl. 3 masc.	ܐܬܝܗܒܘ	* ܢܬܝܗܒܘܢ	---	---	ܡܬܝܗܒܝܢ
pl. 3 fem.	* ܐܬܝܗܒ	* ܢܬܝܗܒܢ	---	---	* ܡܬܝܗܒܢ
pl. 2 masc.	* ܐܬܝܗܒܬܘܢ	* ܬܬܝܗܒܘܢ	* ܐܬܝܗܒܘ	---	---
pl. 2 fem.	* ܐܬܝܗܒܬܝܢ	* ܬܬܝܗܒܢ	* ܐܬܝܗܒܝܢ	---	---
pl. 1 com.	* ܐܬܝܗܒܢ	* ܢܬܝܗܒ	---	---	---
	Infinitive:	* ܡܬܝܗܒܘ			

TABLE 48. The verb ܣܠܩ, No. 134

Form: P^c^al	Perfect	Imperfect	Imperative	Act. Part.	Pass. Part.
sing. 3 masc.	ܣܠܩ	ܢܣܩ	---	ܣܠܩ	*
sing. 3 fem.	ܣܠܩܬ	ܬܣܩ	---	ܣܠܩܐ	*
sing. 2 masc.	* ܣܠܩܬ	ܬܣܩ	ܣܩ	---	---
sing. 2 fem.	* ܣܠܩܬܝ	* ܬܣܩܝܢ	* ܣܩܝ	---	---
sing. 1 com.	ܣܠܩܬ	* ܐܣܩ	---	---	---
pl. 3 masc.	ܣܠܩܘ	ܢܣܩܘܢ	---	ܣܠܩܝܢ	*
pl. 3 fem.	ܣܠܩ	* ܢܣܩܢ	---	ܣܠܩܢ	*
pl. 2 masc.	* ܣܠܩܬܘܢ	* ܬܣܩܘܢ	ܣܩܘ	---	---
pl. 2 fem.	* ܣܠܩܬܝܢ	* ܬܣܩܢ	* ܣܩܝܢ	---	---
pl. 1 com.	ܣܠܩܢ	* ܢܣܩ	---	---	---
	Infinitive:	* ܡܣܩ			

Other Forms. Ethpa^cc^al occurs in ܐܣܬܠܩ (perf. s. 3 masc).

TABLE 49.

Form: Af‪ᶜ‬el	Perfect	Imperfect	Imperative	Act. Part.	Pass. Part.
sing. 3 masc.	ܐܰܩܶܡ	ܢܩܺܝܡ	---	ܡܩܺܝܡ	ܡܩܳܡ *
sing. 3 fem.	ܐܰܩܺܝܡܰܬ *	ܬܩܺܝܡ *	---	ܡܩܺܝܡܳܐ *	ܡܩܳܡܳܐ *
sing. 2 masc.	ܐܰܩܺܝܡܬ *	ܬܩܺܝܡ *	ܐܰܩܶܡ *	---	---
sing. 2 fem.	ܐܰܩܺܝܡܬܝ *	ܬܩܺܝܡܺܝܢ *	ܐܰܩܺܝܡܝ *	---	---
sing. 1 com.	ܐܰܩܺܝܡܶܬ *	ܐܰܩܺܝܡ *	---	---	---
pl. 3 masc.	ܐܰܩܺܝܡܘ *	ܢܩܺܝܡܘܢ *	---	ܡܩܺܝܡܺܝܢ	ܡܩܳܡܺܝܢ *
pl. 3 fem.	ܐܰܩܺܝܡ *	ܢܩܺܝܡܳܢ	---	ܡܩܺܝܡܳܢ *	ܡܩܳܡܳܢ *
pl. 2 masc.	ܐܰܩܺܝܡܬܘܢ *	ܬܩܺܝܡܘܢ *	ܐܰܩܺܝܡܘ *	---	---
pl. 2 fem.	ܐܰܩܺܝܡܬܶܝܢ *	ܬܩܺܝܡܳܢ *	ܐܰܩܺܝܡܶܝܢ *	---	---
pl. 1 com.	ܐܰܩܺܝܡܢ *	ܢܩܺܝܡ	---	---	---
Infinitive:	ܡܩܳܡܽܘ *				

TABLE 50. The verb ܩܰܝܶܡ, No. 62

Form: Pai‪ᶜ‬el	Perfect	Imperfect	Imperative	Act. Part.	Pass. Part.
sing. 3 masc.	ܩܰܝܶܡ	ܢܩܰܝܶܡ	---	ܡܩܰܝܶܡ	ܡܩܰܝܰܡ
sing. 3 fem.	ܩܰܝܡܰܬ	ܬܩܰܝܶܡ *	---	ܡܩܰܝܡܳܐ	ܡܩܰܝܡܳܐ
sing. 2 masc.	ܩܰܝܶܡܬ	ܬܩܰܝܶܡ	ܩܰܝܶܡ	---	---
sing. 2 fem.	ܩܰܝܶܡܬܝ *	ܬܩܰܝܡܺܝܢ	ܩܰܝܶܡܝ *	---	---
sing. 1 com.	ܩܰܝܡܶܬ	ܐܶܩܰܝܶܡ	---	---	---
pl. 3 masc.	ܩܰܝܶܡܘ	ܢܩܰܝܡܘܢ	---	ܡܩܰܝܡܺܝܢ	ܡܩܰܝܡܺܝܢ *
pl. 3 fem.	ܩܰܝܶܡ *	ܢܩܰܝܡܳܢ *	---	ܡܩܰܝܡܳܢ *	ܡܩܰܝܡܳܢ
pl. 2 masc.	ܩܰܝܶܡܬܘܢ	ܬܩܰܝܡܘܢ	ܩܰܝܶܡܘ	---	---
pl. 2 fem.	ܩܰܝܶܡܬܶܝܢ *	ܬܩܰܝܡܳܢ *	ܩܰܝܶܡܶܝܢ *	---	---
pl. 1 com.	ܩܰܝܶܡܢ	ܢܩܰܝܶܡ	---	---	---
Infinitive:	ܡܩܰܝܳܡܽܘ *				

Other Forms. Ethpai‪ᶜ‬al occurs in ܐܶܬܩܰܝܰܡ (perf. s. 3 masc), ܐܶܬܩܰܝܡܶܬ (perf. s. 1 c.), and ܬܶܬܩܰܝܰܡ (impf. s. 3 f.).

Section 7:
English Index

Sequence.

The list is arranged in English alphabetical order.

Format.

Each entry gives an English word followed by reference number(s) which corresponds to the Syriac reference number(s) in Section 1.

English Index: A – atrium

A

abide 183, 817
abiding 746
able, be 42, 507, 700
abode 45
abound, make 217
about 10
abstain from 286
abundance 543, 769
abundantly 218
acceptance 780
accomplish 351
according to 24
accusation 748
accuse 98, 106, 670, 882
accuser 574
act 31
adapt 732
add 484
adhere 348
admonish 773
adulterer 852
adultery, commit 577
adultery 483
advantage 470, 769
advent 494
adversary 307
adverse 824
afar, from 673
affair 400, 739
affirm 730
affliction 266
after 15, 74
afterwards 111, 655
again 101

against 34, 256
age 47
agitation 726
agree 201
ailment 493
alas for! 311
alien 540
alive 194
all 12
allow 92, 471
alms 687
almsgiving 687
alone 139
also 23
altar 495
alter 381, 559
altercation 519
always 294, 564, 822
amazed, be 291
Amen 128
among 20, 514
ancient 785
angel 104
anger 372, 560
angry, be 624
animal 243
animal, young 743
annul 281
anoint 553, 701
Anointed One 35
another 64
answer 120, 279, 374, 820
anxious, be 421
Apocalypse, the 454
apostle 202

apparel 538
apparent 768
apparition 442
appeal to 56, 98, 212
appearance 442
apply 732
appoint 280
apprehend 112
approve 272
approved 490
Aramaean (Syrian) 551
Aramaic, in 826
are 16
argue 725, 730
arouse 356
arrive 251
as 24, 61
as one 478
ascend 134
ascend, make 134
ashamed, be 375
ask 79
aspect 385, 442
assemble 166
assembly 107, 157
assiduously 844
associate 429
assurance 454
astonish 477
astonished, be 477
astray, go 222
astray, lead 222
at 20, 608
at once 263
atrium 657

attain 251
attendance 297
attendant 347, 804
authority 216
avenge 626
avowal 627
awake, be 356
awe 203

B
babe 695
back, the 629
back (of the body) 597
backwards 629
badly 753
bag, leather 759
baptism 413
baptize 215
baptized, be 215
baptizer 664
bare 878
battle 588
bazaar 461
be 3
bear 766
bear (a child) 147
bear 119, 156
beat 434
beaten, be 434, 754
beatitude 337
beautiful 164
because 26
becoming 812
bed 450
before 65, 282, 329, 783
beg 688

beget 147
begin 76
beginning 105, 452, 793
behaviour 807
behind 74, 629
behold 28, 261
behold! 71
being by vocation 790
belief 72
believe 62, 388
believer 319
believing 319
belly 456
beloved 255
benediction 593
benefit 217
betrayer 870
better 174, 488
between 303, 318, 514
beware of 344
bier 450
bind 254
bird 645
birth 661, 770
blame 748
blameless 748
blaspheme 390
blasphemy 576
blemish 699
bless 271
blessedness 337
blessing 593
blind 349
blood 184
boat 325, 363

body 109
bond 550
bondage 742
book 170, 708
border 678
bound 277
boundary 678
bowels 365
bowl 685
boy 214
branch 738
bread 181
break 394
break out against 830
break (bread) 609
breath 40
breath of life 46
bridegroom 660
bright 642
bring 18
bring in 73
bring near 77
brother 54
build 315
building 552
burn 422
burst 830
bury 646
but 6, 21, 403
but rather 21
buy 231
by 20

C
call 56
called 790

calling 884
calm 650
calumniator 574
candlestick 779
cane 789
captain 680
captain of a thousand 563
care of, take 344
careful, be 421
carry 766
carry, make 766
cast 133, 373
cast out, make 49
cause 399
cease 354, 572
celebrate (a feast) 31
centurion 489
certain (one) 768
cessation 650
chain 550, 794
change 559, 559
charity 687
chastise 260
chief 50
chiefs 105
child 695
choke 762
choose 331
chosen 490
Christ 35
church 157
circle 518
circumcise 554
circumcision 396
city 90

clean 482
cleanse 239
cleave to 348
close (a door) 112
closed 797
clothe 302, 621
clothed, be 302
clothing 538
cloud 449
coat 815
cock 751
collect (tribute or tax) 331
colt 743
come 18, 77
comfort 441, 504
coming 494
command 137
commandment 192
commend 186, 848
commit 848
commotion 726, 749
communion 649
companion 429, 860
company at a meal 707
compare 233
comparison 710
compassion 809
compassion, have 149
complete 99, 116
completed, be 99
comprehend 594
comrade 429
conceal 411
conception 219
concerning 10

condemn 312
condemned, be 312
condescension 663
conduct 191, 491, 807
conduct oneself 193
confess 208
confession 627
confidence 889
confident, be 513
confine 678
confirm 596
conflict 838
confused, be 333
congregation 157
congruous 812
conscience 463
consecrate 474
consider 162, 532, 674
constant 843
constantly 844
constrain 341
constructed, be 835
consume 106
consummation 648
contempt, treat w/ 888
contend 730
contention 519
contest 838
continue 817
contradiction 519
contrary 824
convict 773
convince 252
corner 526
corrupt 381

corruption 579
council 223
counsel 339, 506, 819
countenance 385
country 70, 154
court 657
cousin 841
covenant 408
cover 411
covet 500
craft 603
create 654
creation 515
creature, living 243
cross 466
cross over 163
crossing 458
crowd 107
crown 582
crucify 299
cry aloud 212
cry out 727
cultivate 253
cultivator 606
cunning (words) 377
cup 398
cure 690
cured, be 690
curse 600
custom 784
cut 554
cut down 394
cut off 394

D

dance 887

danger 832
dare 602
dark 292
dark, grow 810
darken 810
darkened, be 810
darkness (dark place) 292
daughter 343
dawn 757
day 51
daybreak 510
daytime 418
dead, be 110
dead 140
dead, place of the 675
deaf 633
death, put to 110
death 144
debate 725
debtor 327
decay 579
deceit 603
deceive 222
deception 857
declare 156
decorous 812
decrease 614
decree 192
deed 102, 739
deep 877
defect 729
defend 49
defense 820
deficient 534
defile 544

defiled 410
delay 798
deliberate 248, 339
deliver 286, 547
deliver up 99
deliverance 509
delivered up, be 99
deliverer 829
delude 222
demon 314, 407
denarius 555
deny 334, 662
depart 43, 286, 387
depth 877
deride 628
descend 161
desert 583
desire 69, 173, 500, 611
desolation 420
despise 566, 622, 723, 888
destroy 196, 381
devil 407
die 110
different 821
diligence 855
disciple 68
disease 493, 696
disperse 575
dispute 519, 725
distant 511
distribute 317
diverse 821
divide 317, 317
division 787
do 285

doctrine 250
dominion 216
door 220
doubt 317
dove 859
drag 434
dragon 719
draw 434
dress 538
drink, give to 716
drink 213
drown 762
drunk, become 885
dry up 767
due 812
dumb 633
dwell 278
dweller 827

E
each one 27
eager, be 764
ear 324
earnestness 855
earth 70, 858
earthquake 726
eat 106, 446
eat a meal 76
edge 200
edict 192
edification 552
effect 285
eight 795
elder 205
elect 331, 490
elevate 299

else 63
empty 825
empty, make 567
emulation 632
encampment 872
encounter 799
encourage 441, 580, 863
encouragement 504
end 345, 648
endeavor 774
endurance 412
endure 156
enemy 367
enter 73
entirely 12
entrusted, be 848
envy 632
epistle 439
equal, be 201
erect 299
err 222, 360
error 545, 857
escort 864
especially 218
establish 36, 126, 388, 528
eternity 47
eunuch 865
even 23
even if 402
evening 589
event 739
ever 564, 822
every 12
every one 185
everyday 536

everything 206
evil 103
exalt 274
examine 532, 846
exceedingly 218
excelling 174
excessive 174
exemplar 258
exercised, be 49
exhort 580
expect 448
expedient 488
experience 634
explain 435
exposed 878
expound 525
extinguish 851
extreme 288
eye 122

F
face 130, 385
faith 72
faithful 865
fall 121
false 368
falsely, speak 849
family 228, 661
famine 698
far 511
far place 673
fashion 752
fast 499
fasten 254
father 41
favour 123

fear 155
fear, cause to 155
fear 203
feast 498, 707
feast, wedding 704
feasts 659
fed, be 156
feed 106, 590, 891
feel 382
feeling 634
fellow servant 860
fellowship 649
festival 498
festivity 704
fetter 550
field 246
fig 548
fig tree 548
fight 77, 774
fighting 588
figure 667, 752
fill 116
filthy 410
find 42
fire 210
first 169
fish 436
fitting 272
five 305
flee 340
flesh 138
flock 644
flow 260
follow 348, 395
food 447, 740

fool 219
foolish 605
foolishness 545
foot 176
for 1, 17, 153
forbid 485
force 125, 788
fore 169
foreign 540
foreigner 761
forget 222
forgive 92
forgiveness 592
form 258, 752
formerly 282, 329
fornication 483
fornicator 852
forty 479
foundation 527
four 267
fragment 883
frailty 861
free 595
free, set 731
freedman 595
freedom 853
friend 429, 438
frightened, be 834
from 4
from this time 778
fruit (of the vine) 770
fruit 211
fruits, first 452
fulfil 351
fulfilment 648

full, be 604
fulness 648
furthermore 101
fury 560

G

gain 217, 769
Galilean 847
garment, linen 815
garment 283, 457
gate 220
gather 166, 331
gathering (of persons) 107
Gehenna 802
generation 228
Gentile 551, 761
Gentiles 57
gentle 539
gentleness 724
gift 320, 414
gird 328
girl 214
give 37
give back 279
glad, be 221
gladden 221
gladness 259, 724
glorification 195
glorify 186, 326
glory 179, 195, 358
glorying 502
go 43
go around 362
go away 286
go before 296
go out (fire) 851

English Index: *go out - hypocrisy*

go out 49	*happening* 739	*here and there* 778
go up 134	*happiness* 337	*hidden, be* 522
God 13	*hard* 671	*hide* 411, 522
god, a 13	*harlot* 758	*hide oneself* 522
God forbid 631	*harlotry* 483	*high, be* 274
godless 761	*harm, suffer* 658	*high* 366
gold 352	*harm* 658	*highway* 165
good 93, 164	*harvest* 763	*hill* 249
goodness 123	*hate* 350	*hinder* 485, 890
goods 587	*he* 7	*hold* 112
Gospel 313, 417	*he who* 52	*hold on to* 730
governor 556	*head* 105, 833	*holder* 797
grace 123	*heal* 227	*holiness* 178, 711
graciousess 123	*healthy* 558	*holy* 127
graft 521	*heap up* 646	*homage, pay* 264
grafted, be 521	*hear* 38	*honour* 346, 358
grave 473	*hear, cause to* 38	*hope* 162, 270
great 50	*hearing* 871	*horn* 526
great, be 425	*heart* 113	*horse* 886
greater 174	*heathen* 761	*hour* 131
greatness 647	*heaven* 60	*house* 45
ground 70	*heavy* 492	*housetop* 839
grow up 386	*heavy, be* 346	*how* 61
guard 136, 804	*heavy, make* 346	*how many?* 229
guest 653	*Hebrew, in* 826	*how much?* 229
guile 603	*hedge* 688	*human* 83
guilt 603	*heed, take* 344	*humble, be* 584
H	*heed* 175	*humble* 539, 584
habitation 620	*heir* 635	*humility* 663
hair 643	*hell* 802	*hunger* 537, 698
half 880	*help* 470, 868	*hurry* 834
hand 53	*helper* 868	*hurt* 658
hand, at 287	*hence* 75, 298	*husband* 58, 330
handmaid 845	*henceforth* 284	*husbandman* 606
happen 42	*here* 298, 720, 814	*hypocrisy* 780

hypocrite 130
hypocrite, be a 85
I
I 8
i.e., that is to say 332
idea 219
idle, be 281
idol 472
if 33, 275
illumine 435
illumined 642
image 258, 472, 667
imagination 721
immediately 263
impious 836
impress 856
impure 410, 811
impurity 694
in 20, 419
incense (censings) 531
incite 580
incline toward 175
increase 386, 425, 484
increase, cause 386
indeed 636
indignation 372
individual (self) 669
infant 695
inferior, be 614
infirm 431
infirmity 493, 861
inhabitant 827
inherit 598
inheritance 617
iniquity 364

inquire 79
inquire into 59
instead 153
instruct 260
instruction 250
interpret 525
into 20
is 7, 16
is not 89
island 683
it 7
it suffices 562
ivory 715
J
jealous, be 764
jealousy 632
jealousy, provoke 764
jealousy 765
Jew 96
journey 260
journeying 165
joy 259
joyfully, live 553
judge 150, 455
judgement 172
judgement-seat 801
just 316, 505
justice 244
justify 272
justness 353
K
keep 136
kill 145
kin 661
kindle 112

kindled, be 167
kindliness 724
kindness 123
king 135
kingdom 114
kinsman 841
kinswoman 841
kiss 737
knee 681
kneel 271
knock 823
know 32
knowledge 306, 599
known 768
known, make 32
L
labour 253, 468, 744
labourer 745
lack 692
lacking 534
lake 813
lamb 359
lamp 652
lamp-stand 779
land 70
land, dry 858
language 273
last 288
lasting 746
law 87
lawful 290
lawyer 224
lead 191, 434
lead about 362
lead away 491

English Index: *learn* - *money*

learn 129	*long*, make 781	*manner of life* 807
least 247	*long ago* 618	*many* 44
leave 92	*long suffering* 818	*marketplace* 461
leaven 691	*look* 261	*martyr* 426
left 741	*look for* 448	*marvel* 291, 676
leisure 782	*loosen* 76	*master* 25, 50, 330, 610
lend 79	*loosened, be* 76	*matter* 400, 739
less, be 614	*lord* 25, 330	*mature* 351, 803
lesson 884	*lose* 196, 692	*measure* 735
lest 197	*loss* 529	*meditate* 674
let out 112	*loud voice* 366	*meekness* 663
let it not be 631	*love* 143, 149, 167	*meet* 799
letter 439	*lovingkindness* 143	*member* 369
liar 368	*lowliness* 663	*mention* of, make 397
liberty 853	*lowly* 539	*mercy* 809
lie 849	*lucre* 769	*mercy*, have 149, 149
life 108	*lull* 650	*mercy* 365
life-giving 638	*luminaries* 642	*merrily*, live 553
lift up 299	*lust* 475, 500, 611, 634	*merry, be* 553
light 642	**M**	*message* 313
light, bring to 435	*Macedonian* 869	*messenger* 104
light 237, 242, 652	*mad, be* 387	*Messiah* 35
like as 549	*Magdelene* 775	*middle* 432, 880
liken to 233	*magistrate* 680	*midst* 432
likewise 517	*magistrates* 290, 591	*mighty* 557, 854
limb 369	*maid* 214	*mighty work* 125
line 228	*maintain* 112	*mina (monetary unit)* 866
linen sheet 816	*majesty* 358	*mind* 219, 599, 721
little 237, 247	*make* 31, 654	*minister* 265, 347
live 117	*male* 805	*ministration* 297
live, make 117	*man* 58	*miraculous* token 207
living 194	*man, young* 585	*mistake* 857
lo! 71	*manifest* 180	*mock* 628
lodge 76	*mankind* 30	*moment* 497
loins 597	*manner* 784	*money* 361

English Index: *monster - pass over*

monster 719
month 535
moon 874
more 174
morning 510
mother 190
mount 835
mountain 249
mourn 887
mouth 200
much 44, 93
multiply 425
multitude 107, 543
murder 831
murmur 747
mute 633
myriad 791
mystery 440
N
naked 878
name 78
narrate 428
nation 57, 840
nationality 661
nature 619
Nazarene 542
near 53, 256, 608
near, draw 77
near, bring 77
near 287
necessity 788
need 523, 729
neglect 723, 734
neighbour 287, 429
net 641

nevertheless 403
new 268
next 111
night 241
nine 679
no 2, 393
noble 595
not 2, 393
not even 199
notable 768
nourish 386, 891
now 100, 284, 636
number 601
O
O! 613
oath, take an 392
oath 600
obedience 871
obey 38
observe 136
obtain 623
occasion 399
occupation 879
offend 706
offended, be 424
offense 717
offer 77
offering 414
officer 804
offspring 770
Oh! 613
oil 702
ointment 531, 702
old 785
olive 578

Olives, Mount of 578
on 10
one 27
one, certain 27
one another 630
one hundred 486
only 139
open 204
opportunity 497
oppose 98
opposite to 256
oppression 266
or 63
outer 756
outside 209
overcome 409
overtake 594
owe 312
own 88
ox 718
P
pain 696
pallet 450
parable 321, 710
paralytic 703
part (of a ship) 516
part 640
partake (of) 521
partaker, be 462
partaker 713
participation 649
partner 713
partnership 649
party 516
pass over 163

English Index: *passion - read*

passion 634
Passover, Feast of 451
pastor 571
patience 412
patient, be 781
pattern 258
pay 406
peace 118, 714
pen 789
people 30, 57, 840
perdition 529
perfect 351, 803
perform 31
perhaps 618, 636
peril 832
period 86
perish 196
permit 471
permitted 290
persecute 395
perseverance 855
person 30, 83, 385, 669
persuade 252
petition 755
Pharisee 171
pity 808
place 94, 154, 235
place, far 673
place 133
plague 496
plan 674
planet 443
plant 736
platter 685
play 428

pleasantness 724
please 416
ploughshare 693
poor 371
portion 640, 787
portrait 667
possession 587
potentate 557
pour out 480
power 125, 216
praise 179, 186, 195
pray 175
prayer 309, 755
preach 156, 187
preached, be 187
precept 192
precious 492
precious, be 346
prefect 556
prefer 217
prepare 148, 528
presence-bread 130
present, be 98
preserver 638
price 684
pride oneself 326
priest 146, 444
priesthood, high 647
prisoner 277
proclaimed, be 187
prodigy 676
profane 761
profess 208
profit 769
profit, be of 470

profitable 488
prolonged, be 781
promise 208, 339, 370, 750
proper, it 225
property 587
prophecy 565
prophesy 433
prophet 115
prophetess 115
proportion 735
prostitute 758
prove 355, 532
proverb 321
provoke 624
prudent 377
publican 469
pure 482
pursue 286
put 94, 133
put off 354
put on 302

Q

queen 135
quench 851
question 59, 725
quickly 404
quiet, be 572
quiet 572
quietness 650

R

rabbi 610
rain 777
rather than 63
reach 251
read 56

reading 884
ready, make 234
realm 114
reap 561
reasoning 506
rebuke 430, 581, 773
receive 85, 98
receptacle 283
reckon 248
recline to eat 322
recline, cause to 322
recognize 32
recompense 378, 406
recreation 782
rectitude 244
redemption 509
reed 789
refresh 354
refuse 334
region 154
reign 114, 339
reject 566, 662
rejoice 221
rejoice, be 553
release 592
remain 183, 817
remain over 217
remainder 357
remaining 746
remember 383, 397
remember, cause to 383
remind 397
remission 592
remote 511
remove 387

rend 830
repent 374
repentance 512
repose 782
reprove 430
reproved, be 773
repudiation 592
require 59, 626
rescue 286
resemble 233
reserve 136
residue 357
resist 256
respite 154
rest 354
rest, give 354
rest 357, 782
restore 528
restored, be 528
restrain 485
resurrection 379
return 193, 279, 374
reveal 180
revelation 454
revile 881
reward 406
rich 384
rich, grow 786
rich, make 786
riches 546
ride 835
ride, make 835
right, it is 225
right 293
right, it is 272

righteous 316, 505
righteousness 244, 353
riot 749
rise 757
rise, make 757
rise 36
river 665
road 165
robust 557
rock 236, 712
rod 591
roll 708
Roman 672
roof 839
root 569
rough 671
ruler 680
rulers 290
run 323
S
Sabbath 238
sacrifice 481
Sadducee 686
sadness 862
saint 127
salutation 118
salute 79, 118
salvation 108, 509
Samaritan 573
sanctification 711
sanctify 474
sanctuary 152, 178
sandal 867
Satan 307
satisfied, be 604

satisfy 604	serve 265	sleep 391
save 117, 286	service 297, 742	smitten, be 754
Saviour 638, 829	set (on fire) 422	smoke 796
say 5	seven 177	smooth 201
scare away 575	shaken, be 333	snatch 616
scatter 575	shaking 726	so 389, 517
sceptre 591	shame 375, 800	soil 70
scourge 434	sheep, young 359	soldier 524, 530
scribe 224	sheep 508	solicitous, be 421
Scripture 170	Sheol 675	something 39
scroll 708	shepherd 571	son 22
sea 160	shewbread 181	sorely 753
seal 733, 856	shine 435, 757	sorrow 445
search 846	ship 325, 363	sorrowfulness 862
season 86, 497	shoe 867	sorry, make 445
seat 126, 269	shorten 445	soul 46
seat at a meal 707	show 182	sound 558
sect 516	sick, be 423	sow 300
see 28	sick 431	space or room, available 154
seed 301	sickness 493, 861	spare 808
seek for 59	side 516	speak 5, 55
seemly 812	sign 207	spend 575
seize 616	silence 503, 650	spirit 40
self 46	silent, keep 503	spirit, evil 314
sell 231	silver 361, 873	spot 699
send 82, 612	similitude 258, 321	spread 201
sent one 202	sin 168, 198, 360	square 461
sentence (of judge) 172	sink 215	staff 591
separate 280	sinner 304	stamp 733, 856
separation 787	sister 520	stand 36
sepulchre 405, 473	sit 126	stand, cause to 36
serpent 728	six 476	star 443
servant, female bond- 845	skull 833	steadfast 257
servant 132, 347, 524, 804	sky 60	steal 656
serve, make 253	slaughter 693, 831	steer 718

English Index: *still - tire*

still 427
still, be 503
stir up 333
stir 333
stir up 625
stock 228
stone 236, 570
stop 572
store 487
straight, be 607
strange 540
stranger 653
strangle 762
street 461
strength 125
strengthen 388, 596
stretch out 607, 771
strife 519
strike 328, 774
strive 730, 774
stroke 496
strong 557, 558, 671, 854
strong, be 388
struck, be 754
stumble, make 424
stumble 890
stumbling block 717
subdue 31
subject 31
substance 587, 669
suddenly 650
suffer 382
suffering 634, 696
suffice 507
sufficient, be 507

sun 401
supper 659
support 322, 891
suppose 162
surround 688
surroundings 518
sustenance 740
swallow up 754
swear 392
swear, make 392
swift 237
swine 689
sword 693, 705, 875
symposium 704
synagogue 223

T

tabernacle 620
table 586
take 85, 98, 112, 191, 491
take up 119
taking 780
talent 772
tarry 798
taste 521
tax collector 469
teach 129
teacher 335
teaching 250
tear 806
tedious 734
temple 152
tempt 355
temptation 541
ten 459
ten thousand 791

tend 590
tent 620
testament 408
testify 151
testimony 245
thanks, give 208
thanksgiving 627
that 14
the Cross 466
then 111, 637
there 95
therefore 75, 284, 637
thief 615
thing 400
think 162, 248, 336, 674
third 677
thirsty, be 666
thirty 837
this 9
this is he 240
thorn 697
those 14
thou 11
thought 219, 506, 721
thousand 310
three 142
throne 269
through 53
throw 373
thunder 792
thus 67
tidings, good 313
tiller 606
time 86, 497
tire 468

tired, be 734	*tumult* 749	*vain* 825
to 1, 34	*tunic* 815	*vainglory* 502
to-day 338	*turn* out 3	*vainly* 876
together 478	*turn* 193, 621	*valid* 746
toil 468, 744	*turn*, cause to 279	*various* 821
tomb 405, 473	*turn away from* 163	*vaunting* 502
tomorrow 776	*tusk* 715	*verily* 128
tongue 273	*twelve* 226	*verity* 415
tooth 715	*twenty* 828	*vessel* 283
torment 651	*two* 97	*vessel, sailing* 363
touch 77	*type* 258	*victim* 481
toward 34	**U**	*village* 246
town 90	*uncircumcision* 568	*vineyard* 467
trade 879	*unclean* 410, 811	*violence* 788
train 725	*uncleaness* 694	*virgin* 682
traitor 870	*under* 230	*virtue* 125
trample 850	*understand*, make 308	*visit* 285
tranquility 714	*understand* 308	*visitation* 739
transgress 163	*understanding* 599	*vocation* 884
transmitted, be 491	*ungodly* 836	*voice* 124
transmute 559	*unguent* 531, 702	*void* 825
treasure 487	*unjust* 709	*void*, make 567
tree 464, 668	*unrighteousness* 364	*vomit* 374
trial 541	*until* 91, 437	**W**
tribe 228, 591	*upright* 505	*wait* 817
tribulation 266	*uprightness* 244, 353	*wake up* 356
tribunal 801	*uproar* 749	*walk* 158
trickery 603	*urge* 341	*wander* 222, 688
trouble 333, 625	*use* 732	*want* 729
true 257	*useful*, be 732	*war* 588
truly 380, 389	*utensil* 283	*warn* 344
trust in 62	*utterance* 343	*was* 3
trust 889	**V**	*wash* 501
truth 189, 415	*vacant* 825	*washing* 413
try 355	*vagrancy* 518	*waste* 529

watch 356
water 188, 716
way 165
ways 807
weak, be 423
weak (in faith) 431
weakness 861
wealth 546
wealthy 384
weary, be 734
weep 342
well 164
what 19, 66, 81
what is this? 639
wheat 760
when 15
when? 276
whence? 465
where 159
where is (he)? 842
which 19
while 15, 437
white 533
who 19
who, he 14
who 52
who is this? 141
whole 12, 558
why 66, 262, 295
wick 652
wicked 709, 836
wickedness 722
widow 453
wife 80
wilderness 420, 583

will 69, 173
wind 40
wine 376
wineskin 759
wipe 201
wisdom 289
wise 377
with 20, 29, 608
withdraw 434
wither 767
wither, cause to 767
within 419
witness 151, 426
woe! 311
woman 80
womb 456
wonder 676
wood 668
word 48, 343, 460
work 102, 253, 879
worker 745
world 47
worship 264
worshipper 524
worthy 201
wound 496
wrap 362
wrath 372, 560
wreath 582
write 84
writing 170
wrong 103, 662, 706
wrong-doing 545, 722

Y
yea 389

year 232
yet 6, 403, 427
young man 585
youth 214, 585

Z
zeal 765
zest 855
zone

Section 8:
Alphabetical Index

Sequence.

The list is arranged in Syriac alphabetical order.

Format.

Each entry gives a Syriac word followed by a reference number which corresponds to the Syriac reference number in Section 1.

ܐܒܐ 41
ܐܒܝ 196
ܐܒܢܐ 529
ܐܒܘܢܐ 838
ܐܓܪܐ 406
ܐܓܪܐ 839
ܐܓܪܬܐ 439
ܐܕܢܐ 324
ܐܘ 613
ܐܘ 63
ܐܘܚܕܢܐ 266
ܐܘܡܢܐ 840
ܐܘܢܓܠܝܘܢ 417
ܐܘܪܚܐ 165
ܐܙܠ 43
ܐܚܐ 54
ܐܚܝ 112
ܐܚܝܐ 797
ܐܚܢܐ 841
ܐܚܕ 798
ܐܚܕܢܐ 288
ܐܚܪܢܐ 64
ܐܝܐ 53
ܐܝܟ 24
ܐܝܟܐ 159
ܐܝܟܘ 842
ܐܝܠܝܢ 61
ܐܝܠܢܐ 464
ܐܝܡܡܐ 465
ܐܝܡܡܐ 418
ܐܝܢ 389
ܐܝܢܐ 19
ܐܝܟܢܐ 358
ܐܝܬ 16
ܐܟܘܬ 549
ܐܟܣܝܐ 478
ܐܟܠ 106
ܐܟܠ ܩܪܨܐ 574
ܐܟܣܢܝܐ 653
ܐܠܐ 21
ܐܠܗܐ 13
ܐܠܘ 275
ܐܠܦܐ 310
ܐܠܦܐ 325
ܐܠܨ 341
ܐܡܐ 190
ܐܡܝܢ 128
ܐܡܝܢܐ 843
ܐܡܝܢܐܝܬ 844
ܐܡܪ 5
ܐܡܪܐ 359
ܐܡܓܐ 845
ܐܡܬܝ 276
ܐܢ 33
ܐܢܐ 8
ܐܢܫܐ 30
ܐܢܬ 11
ܐܢܬܬܐ 80
ܐܣܐ 227
ܐܣܘܪܐ 550
ܐܣܛܪܛܝܘܛܐ 530
ܐܣܝܐ 277
ܐܣܩܡܐ 752
ܐܣܪ 254
ܐܦ 23
ܐܦܐ 130
ܐܦܠܐ 199
ܐܦܝ 402
ܐܪܒܥܐ 267
ܐܪܒܥܝܢ 479
ܐܪܙܐ 440
ܐܪܓܘܢܐ 680
ܐܪܥܐ 551
ܐܪܡܠܬܐ 453
ܐܪܟ 799
ܐܪܟܐ 70
ܐܫܝ 480
ܐܬܐ 207
ܐܬܐ 18
ܐܬܪܐ 154
ܒ 20
ܒܐܪ 575
ܒܗܪ 326
ܒܗܬܐ 375
ܒܗܬܬܐ 800
ܒܘܠܐ 504
ܒܘܪܟܐ 681
ܒܘܪܟܬܐ 593
ܒܙܚ 628
ܒܛܝܠ 281
ܒܛܠ 441
ܒܝܬ 801
ܒܝܢ 514
ܒܝܢܬ 303
ܒܝܬܐ 103
ܒܝܬܝܐܝܬ 753
ܒܝܬܘܬܐ 722
ܒܟܝ 318
ܒܟܝܬܐ 45
ܒܟܐ 342
ܒܟܠܗܘܢ 139
ܒܟܠ 754
ܒܢܐ 315
ܒܢ̈ܝܐ 552
ܒܟܐ 723

724 ܚܩܣܩܘܐܐ	17 ܚܒ	391 ܘܫܘ
553 ܚܩܡ	180 ܚܠܐ	806 ܘܨܚܟܐ
531 ܚܩܡܟܐ	847 ܚܟܚܟܢܐ	291 ܘܚܙ
138 ܚܩܙܐ	454 ܚܚܢܢܐ	150 ܐܘ
629 ܚܓܗܚܙܘ	803 ܚܩܡܙܐ	757 ܘܢܣ
59 ܚܕܐ	351 ܚܨܕ	851 ܘܟܘ
755 ܚܘܕܘܐܐ	656 ܚܠܒ	594 ܘܩܘ
330 ܚܕܠܐ	615 ܚܠܢܟܐ	725 ܘܙܡ
367 ܚܚܕܓܓܐ	848 ܚܠܠܐ	657 ܘܙܢܐ
846 ܚܪܐ	481 ܘܓܣܐ	71 ܗܐ
614 ܚܪܘ	191 ܘܓܕ	556 ܩ ܚܨܕܢܐ
532 ܚܛܐ	849 ܘܓܠܐ	369 ܗܙܘܚܐ
22 ܚܕܐ	368 ܘܓܠܐ	7 ܗܘ
654 ܚܕܐ	352 ܘܘܓܐ	14 ܗܘ
756 ܚܕܢܐ	235 ܘܘܚܐ	3 ܗܘܐ
515 ܚܕܙܐܐ	850 ܘܣ	332 ܗܘܢܘ
271 ܚܕܘ	155 ܘܫܠ	240 ܗܘܢܘ
403 ܚܕܡ	203 ܘܣܚܟܐ	807 ܗܘܩܟܐ
83 ܚܕܢܛܐ	804 ܘܣܡܐ	111 ܗܢܡ
343 ܚܕܪܐܐ	407 ܘܡܐ	152 ܗܢܠܐ
682 ܚܘܡܚܟܐ	88 ܘܣܠ	62 ܗܢܫܡ
74 ܚܘܙܘ	6 ܘܡ	72 ܗܣܚܢܐܐ
655 ܚܘܙܘܩ	172 ܘܣܢܐ	517 ܗܥܓܐ
331 ܚܙܐ	455 ܘܢܢܐ	75 ܗܩܨܠܐ
516 ܚܙܚܐ	555 ܘܣܢܙܐ	67 ܗܩܛܢܐ
490 ܚܓܣܐ	408 ܘܢܐܩܐ	158 ܗܟܘ
58 ܚܓܙܐ	239 ܘܗܐ	9 ܗܢܐ
390 ܚܒܘ	482 ܘܣܒܐ	193 ܘܩܘ
802 ܚܟܘܢܐ	397 ܘܒܕ	658 ܗܘ
419 ܚܟܡ	805 ܘܓܚܐ	298 ܗܘܙܢܐ
576 ܚܟܘܙܒܐ	197 ܘܚܚܛܐ	100 ܗܢܡܐ
577 ܚܛ	184 ܘܨܚܐ	311 ܗܡ
396 ܚܝܐܘܢܐܐ	233 ܘܨܚܐ	225 ܗܠܐ
554 ܚܝܐܘ	258 ܘܨܚܘܐܐ	685 ܐܟܘܕܐ
683 ܚܝܐܘܢܐܐ	684 ܘܨܡܢܐ	231 ܐܒܣ

ܙܒܢܐ 86
ܙܕܘܩܝܐ 686
ܙܕܩܐ 316
ܙܕܝܩܘܬܐ 353
ܙܗܐ 272
ܙܗܝܪܐ 687
ܙܗܪ 344
ܙܘܥܐ 726
ܙܚܝܐ 578
ܙܟܐ 409
ܙܢܝܐ 852
ܙܢܝܘܬܐ 483
ܙܢܝܬܐ 758
ܙܥ 333
ܙܥܘܪܐ 247
ܙܥܡ 727
ܙܦܐ 759
ܙܩܝܦܐ 466
ܙܩܦ 299
ܙܪܥ 300
ܙܪܥܐ 301
ܚܐܪܐ 595
ܚܐܪܘܬܐ 853
ܚܒ 167
ܚܒܝܒܐ 255
ܚܒܠ 381
ܚܒܠܐ 579
ܚܒܪܐ 429
ܚܕ 27
ܚܕܘܪܐ 630
ܚܕܘܬܐ 259
ܚܕܝ 221
ܚܕܪ 688
ܚܕܪܐ 518
ܚܕܬܐ 268
ܚܘܐ 182
ܚܘܒ 312
ܚܘܒܐ 143
ܚܘܝܐ 728
ܚܘܣ 808
ܚܘܪ 261
ܚܘܪܐ 533
ܚܘܪܒܐ 420
ܚܙܐ 28
ܚܙܘܐ 442
ܚܙܝܪܐ 689
ܚܛܐ 360
ܚܛܗܐ 168
ܚܛܝܐ 304
ܚܛܝܬܐ 198
ܚܛܦ 616
ܚܛܝܦܐ 760
ܚܝܐ 117
ܚܝ̈ܐ 194
ܚܝܬܐ 108
ܚܝܒܐ 327
ܚܝܘܬܐ 243
ܚܝܠ 596
ܚܝܠܐ 125
ܚܝܠܬܢܐ 557
ܚܟܝܡܐ 377
ܚܟܡܬܐ 289
ܚܠܡܐ 558
ܚܠܡ 690
ܚܠܦ 559
ܚܠܦ 153
ܚܡܝܪܐ 691
ܚܡܪܐ 376
ܚܡܫܐ 305
ܚܡܬܐ 560
ܚܢܢܐ 809
ܚܢܦܐ 761
ܚܣܡ 762
ܚܣ 631
ܚܣܝܢܐ 854
ܚܣܝܪܐ 534
ܚܣܝܪܘܬܐ 729
ܚܣܡܐ 632
ܚܣܪ 692
ܚܦܛ 580
ܚܦܝܛܘܬܐ 855
ܚܩܠܐ 597
ܚܩܪ 561
ܚܩܪܐ 763
ܚܪܐ 730
ܚܪܒܐ 693
ܚܪ̈ܝܢܐ 519
ܚܪܪ 731
ܚܪܡܐ 633
ܚܪܬܐ 345
ܚܫ 382
ܚܫܐ 634
ܚܫܒ 248
ܚܫܘܒܐ 292
ܚܫܟ 732
ܚܫܡ 810
ܚܫܚܬܐ 659
ܚܬܐ 520
ܚܬܡ 856
ܚܬܢܐ 660
ܛܒܐ 93
ܛܒܥܐ 733
ܛܒ 234
ܛܘܒܐ 337
ܛܘܗܡܐ 661

ܛܘܪܐ 249
ܛܒܘܬܐ 123
ܛܒܠܐ 214
ܛܥܡ 662
ܛܥܢܐ 811
ܛܝ 764
ܛܢܢܐ 765
ܛܢܦܐ 410
ܛܢܦܘܬܐ 694
ܛܠܐ 222
ܛܠܝܘܬܐ 857
ܛܠܡ 521
ܛܠܡ 766
ܛܡܐ 522
ܝܐܝܐ 812
ܝܒܠ 491
ܝܕܥ 767
ܝܕܥܐ 858
ܝܗܒ 208
ܝܘܒܠܐ 768
ܝܘܡ 32
ܝܘܡܢܐ 306
ܝܘܢ 37
ܝܘܪܢܐ 96
ܝܚܝܕܝܐ 250
ܝܚܝܕܐ 51
ܝܚܝܕܝܐ 338
ܝܚܢܐ 859
ܝܚܝܐܢܐ 769
ܝܠܕ 147
ܝܠܕܐ 770
ܝܠܕܘܬܐ 695
ܝܠܦ 129
ܝܡܐ 392
ܝܡܐ 160
ܝܡܝܢܐ 293
ܝܡܝܢܐ 813
ܝܡܡ 484
ܝܣܦ 421
ܝܩܕ 422
ܝܩܕܐ 492
ܝܩܪ 346
ܝܪܚܐ 535
ܝܪܝ 598
ܝܪܬܐ 635
ܝܪܬܘܬܐ 617
ܝܫܥ 771
ܝܬܒ 126
ܝܬܝܪܐ 174
ܝܬܝܪܐܝܬ 218
ܝܬܪ 217
ܟܐ 814
ܟܐܐ 430
ܟܐܒܐ 696
ܟܐܢܐ 505
ܟܐܢܘܬܐ 244
ܟܐܦܐ 236
ܟܒܕ 618
ܟܒܪ 15
ܟܕܘ 562
ܟܘܢܐ 146
ܟܘܟܒܐ 697
ܟܘܟܒܐ 443
ܟܘܡܪܐ 444
ܟܘܢ 581
ܟܘܪܗܢܐ 493
ܟܘܪܣܝܐ 269
ܟܘܬܢܐ 815
ܟܚ 636
ܟܝܢܐ 619
ܟܦܪܐ 772
ܟܘܠ 12
ܟܠܒܝܡ 294
ܟܠܢܘܡ 536
ܟܠܡܢܘܡ 206
ܟܠܐ 485
ܟܠܠܐ 582
ܟܠܠܢܝܐ 563
ܟܠܢܫ 185
ܟܡܐ 229
ܟܡܘܪܐ 223
ܟܢܫ 166
ܟܢܫܐ 107
ܟܢܪܐ 860
ܟܣܐ 773
ܟܣܝܐ 398
ܟܣܦܐ 411
ܟܣܦܐ 361
ܟܦܢ 537
ܟܦܢܐ 698
ܟܦܪ 334
ܟܪܐ 445
ܟܪܗ 423
ܟܪܙ 187
ܟܪܝܗܐ 431
ܟܪܝܗܘܬܐ 861
ܟܪܝܘܬܐ 862
ܟܪܟ 362
ܟܪܣܐ 467
ܟܪܣܐ 456
ܟܫܠ 424
ܟܬܒ 84
ܟܬܒܐ 170
ܟܬܢܐ 816
ܦܠܪ 817

ܦܬܚ 774
ܠ 1
ܠܐ 2
ܠܐܐ 468
ܠܒܒܐ 113
ܠܒܒ 863
ܠܒܘܫܐ 538
ܠܒܪ 209
ܠܒܫ 302
ܠܗ 393
ܠܘܐ 864
ܠܘܩܒܠ 256
ܠܘܩܕܡ 282
ܠܘܬ 34
ܠܚܡܐ 181
ܠܟ 89
ܠܠܝܐ 241
ܠܡܐ 262
ܠܡܢܐ 295
ܠܢܫ 446
ܠܥܡܢܐ 273
ܡܐ 81
ܡܐܐ 486
ܡܐܬܝܘܬܐ 447
ܡܐܢ 734
ܡܐܢܐ 283
ܡܐܡܢܬܐ 494
ܡܒܪܟܬܐ 775
ܡܒܪܢܐ 818
ܡܒܪܚܡܐ 495
ܡܒܪܢܐ 583
ܡܒܪܡ 637
ܡܒܝܢܬܐ 90
ܡܕܡ 39
ܡܕܒܪܐ 599
ܡܗܝܡܢܐ 865
ܡܗܝܡܢܐ 319
ܡܘܗܒܬܐ 320
ܡܘܡܐ 699
ܡܘܠܟܢܐ 370
ܡܘܡܬܐ 600
ܡܘܬ 110
ܡܘܬܐ 144
ܡܚܐ 328
ܡܚܝܐ 263
ܡܚܘܬܐ 496
ܡܚܝܢܐ 638
ܡܚܙ 776
ܡܚܡܣܬܐ 506
ܡܛܐ 251
ܡܛܠ 26
ܡܛܪܐ 777
ܡܝܬܐ 188
ܡܝܬܬܐ 140
ܡܟ 584
ܡܟܐ 778
ܡܟܝܟܐ 539
ܡܟܝܟܘܬܐ 663
ܡܟܝܠ 284
ܡܟܫܦܐ 469
ܡܠܐ 116
ܡܠܐܟܐ 104
ܡܠܟ 339
ܡܠܟܐ 135
ܡܠܟܐ 819
ܡܠܟܘܬܐ 114
ܡܠܠ 55
ܡܠܦܢܐ 335
ܡܠܬܐ 48
ܡܡܠܘܡ 564
ܡܢ 52
ܡܢ 4
ܡܢܐ 66
ܡܢܗ 141
ܡܢܗ 639
ܡܢܝܐ 866
ܡܢܝܢܐ 601
ܡܢܪܬܐ 779
ܡܢܬܐ 640
ܡܣܒܐ 780
ܡܣܬܒܪܢܘܬܐ 412
ܡܣܟܢܐ 371
ܡܣܐܢܐ 867
ܡܥܕܪܢܐ 868
ܡܥܡܕܢܐ 664
ܡܥܡܘܕܝܬܐ 413
ܡܦܩܐ 820
ܡܨܐ 700
ܡܨܝܢܬܐ 641
ܡܨܠܝܬܐ 432
ܡܩܝܘܢܐ 869
ܡܪܚ 602
ܡܪܐ 25
ܡܫܘܚܬܐ 735
ܡܫܚ 701
ܡܫܚܐ 702
ܡܫܚܠܦܐ 821
ܡܫܝܚܐ 35
ܡܫܟܢܐ 620
ܡܫܠܡܢܐ 870
ܡܫܡܠܝܬܐ 871
ܡܫܡܫܢܐ 347
ܡܫܪܐ 703
ܡܫܪܝܬܐ 872
ܡܫܬܘܬܐ 704

ܡܬܐܘܡ 822
ܡܬܠܐ 321
ܢܒܠܐ 433
ܢܒܝܠܐ 115
ܢܒܝܘܬܐ 565
ܢܒܝ 434
ܢܒܥ 781
ܢܘܗܪܐ 642
ܢܗܪ 435
ܢܗܪܐ 665
ܢܗܝܪܐ 242
ܢܚ 354
ܢܘܟܪܝܐ 540
ܢܘܢܐ 436
ܢܘܪܐ 210
ܢܚܬ 161
ܢܚܫܐ 457
ܢܛܪ 136
ܢܣܟܐ 782
ܢܟܠܐ 603
ܢܡܘܣܐ 87
ܢܣܐ 355
ܢܣܒ 85
ܢܣܝܘܢܐ 541
ܢܦܠ 121
ܢܦܩ 49
ܢܦܫܐ 46
ܢܨܒ 736
ܢܨܪܝܐ 542
ܢܩܦ 348
ܢܩܫ 823
ܢܫܩ 737
ܣܐܡܐ 873
ܣܒܪ 604
ܣܒܥ 162
ܣܒܪ 156
ܣܒܪܐ 270
ܣܒܪܬܐ 313
ܣܓܝܐ 425
ܣܓܕ 264
ܣܓܝܐܐ 44
ܣܗܕ 151
ܣܗܕܐ 426
ܣܗܕܘܬܐ 245
ܣܗܕܐ 874
ܣܘܓܐܐ 543
ܣܘܟܐ 738
ܣܘܟܠܢܐ 739
ܣܘܢܢܐ 307
ܣܟ 544
ܣܟܪܢܐ 740
ܣܡܝܐ 487
ܣܡܟܐ 705
ܣܢܐ 448
ܣܥܠ 308
ܣܒܠ 706
ܣܥܠܐ 605
ܣܥܪܘܬܐ 545
ܣܠܐ 566
ܣܩܡ 134
ܣܡ 94
ܣܡܢܐ 349
ܣܡܟ 322
ܣܡܟܐ 707
ܣܡܠܐ 741
ܣܢܐ 350
ܣܢܩ 523
ܣܥܪ 285
ܣܥܪܐ 643
ܣܩܘܒܠܐ 363
ܣܦܣܪܐ 875
ܣܦܩ 507
ܣܦܪܐ 708
ܣܦܪܐ 224
ܣܩܘܒܠܐ 824
ܣܪܝܩܐ 825
ܣܪܝܩܐܝܬ 876
ܣܪܩ 567
ܥܒܕ 31
ܥܒܕܐ 132
ܥܒܕܐ 102
ܥܒܕܘܬܐ 742
ܥܒܪ 163
ܥܒܪܐ 458
ܥܒܪܐܝܬ 826
ܥܓܠ 404
ܥܕ 437
ܥܕܡܐ ܠ 427
ܥܕܠܐ 783
ܥܕܬܐ 91
ܥܕܢܐ 497
ܥܕܥܕܐ 498
ܥܕܪ 470
ܥܕܪܢܐ 157
ܥܗܕ 383
ܥܘܠܐ 709
ܥܘܠܐ 364
ܥܘܡܩܐ 877
ܥܘܕܪܘܬܐ 568
ܥܘܬܪܐ 546
ܥܛܦ 621
ܥܝܢܐ 784
ܥܟܠܐ 743
ܥܠܡܐ 122
ܥܠ 73

ܠܐ 10	ܦܚܝܢܘܬܐ 787	ܪܓܐ 622
ܚܟܡܬܐ 585	ܦܟܣ 253	ܪܘܙܐ 510
ܚܠܡܐ 47	ܦܠܚܢܐ 524	ܪܘܐ 830
ܚܠܒܐ 399	ܦܠܟܢܐ 606	ܡܓܘܙܐ 405
ܠܡ 29	ܦܢܐ 279	ܡܓܠܐ 98
ܠܚܡܐ 57	ܦܣ 471	ܡܓܕ 646
ܠܨܝ 215	ܦܣܩ 394	ܡܓܕܐ 473
ܠܡܘܕܐ 827	ܦܠܠܐ 745	ܡܝܬܐ 329
ܠܡܠܐ 744	ܦܪܐ 547	ܡܛܪܐ 127
ܠܨܕ 278	ܦܪܝܢܐ 451	ܡܛܪܢܘܬܐ 711
ܠܢܐ 120	ܦܨܝ 137	ܡܝܡ 296
ܠܟܐ 644	ܦܩܕܐ 488	ܡܝܡ 65
ܠܫܢܐ 449	ܦܪܘܕܐ 829	ܡܘܕܐ 169
ܠܬܩܐ 459	ܦܪܣܐ 645	ܡܝܣ 474
ܠܬܩܝ 828	ܦܪܩܐ 171	ܡܕܐ 183
ܠܬܩܐ 569	ܦܩܕ 378	ܡܘܪܡܐ 178
ܠܕ 356	ܦܪܙܦܐ 385	ܡܘܙܟܐ 414
ܠܕܠܐ 508	ܦܩܕ 286	ܡܘܡܪܐ 415
ܠܕܒܝܟܢܐ 878	ܦܩܕ 280	ܡܓܕܐ 788
ܠܕܠܐ 450	ܦܩܕܝ 607	ܡܝܠܐ 145
ܠܕܫ 340	ܦܩܩ 525	ܡܚܠܐ 831
ܠܓܕܘ 148	ܦܩܝܠܚܡܐ 460	ܡܚܒܝ 882
ܠܟܕܡܐ 785	ܦܩܪܘܬܐ 586	ܡܢܕܐ 746
ܠܟܕܢܐ 384	ܦܩܣ 204	ܡܢܚܕܐ 379
ܠܓܘ 786	ܦܩܒܕܐ 472	ܡܢܚܐ 668
ܩܘܘܐ 211	ܪܓܠ 69	ܡܠܠܐ 124
ܦܝܡܐ 109	ܪܒܘܬܐ 400	ܡܟܬܒܐ 237
ܦܘܚܡܢܐ 879	ܪܓܢܐ 173	ܡܡ 36
ܦܘܡܐ 200	ܪܗܐ 666	ܡܢܐ 623
ܦܘܬܪܢܐ 192	ܪܝܡ 499	ܡܢܝܢܘܣ 832
ܦܘܙܢܐ 509	ܪܝܣܐ 881	ܡܢܕܡܐ 669
ܦܣ 252	ܪܝܒ 608	ܡܢܓܙܘܢܐ 489
ܦܠܐܠܐ 710	ܪܠܐ 175	ܡܣܝܐ 789
ܦܟܝ 317	ܪܟܕܒܐ 309	ܡܣܢܐ 587
ܦܪܚܝܐ 880	ܪܚܡܐ 667	ܡܟܐ 212

مܐܪܐ 609	ܕܢܣܛܪܐ 511	ܡܘܓܠܣܐ 195
ܡܪܢܐ 883	ܕܢܫܡ 149	ܡܘܓܦܢܐ 592
ܡܐܪ 56	ܕܢܣܩܐ 438	ܡܘܘܙܢܐ 750
ܡܐܪܒ 77	ܕܢܣܩܐ 365	ܡܘܝ 888
ܡܐܪܟܐ 588	ܕܢܩ 747	ܡܘܚܟܢܐ 216
ܡܐܪܢܐ 790	ܕܢܩܠܐ 105	ܡܘܚܟܪ 648
ܡܐܪܬܟܐ 287	ܕܢܩܡܠܐ 452	ܡܘܟܐ 712
ܡܐܪܬܢܠܐ 884	ܕܢܩܨ 835	ܡܘܡܐ 461
ܡܐܪܬܟܠܐ 246	ܕܢܩܡܐ 886	ܡܘܘܢܐ 793
ܡܐܪܢܠܐ 526	ܕܢܩܚܐ 366	ܡܘܐܩ 462
ܡܐܪܙܠܐ 670	ܕܢܩܚܐ 133	ܡܘܐܦܠܐ 713
ܡܐܪܘܒܓܠܐ 833	ܕܢܨܚܐ 589	ܡܘܐܦܩܒܐܠ 649
ܡܐܡܢܠܐ 671	ܕܢܠܐ 674	ܡܢܘܗ 675
ܡܐܡܣܡܠܐ 205	ܕܢܟܐ 590	ܡܘܢܠܐ 714
ܕܐܟܠܐ 50	ܕܢܟܐ 336	ܡܢܡܟܠܐ 794
ܕܟܠܐ 386	ܕܢܚܟܐ 571	ܡܩܣ 42
ܕܟܘܒܐܠ 791	ܕܢܚܣܢܐ 219	ܡܟܣ 612
ܕܟܘܒܐܠ 647	ܕܢܚܨܟܠܐ 792	ܡܟܬ 572
ܕܟܣ 610	ܕܢܩܝ 887	ܡܟܬܠܐ 650
ܕܒ 500	ܕܢܥܡܢܠܐ 748	ܡܟܬܣܠܐ 202
ܕܓ 624	ܕܢܨܟܚܠܐ 836	ܡܟܬܟܠܐ 290
ܕܓܡܝܓܕܠܐ 475	ܕܢܐܘܙܠܐ 314	ܡܟܬܡ 99
ܕܓܠܐܠ 176	ܥܡܐܠܠ 79	ܡܟܟܚܠܐ 118
ܕܓܟܡ 570	ܡܚܣ 186	ܡܩܦܠܐ 78
ܕܓܟܓܐܠ 611	ܡܚܓܠܐ 591	ܡܩܩܢܠܐ 60
ܕܘܐܪܠ 260	ܡܚܓܟܠܐ 177	ܡܩܩܕ 38
ܕܘܘܒ 395	ܡܟܓܕ 92	ܡܩܩܕܢܠܐ 573
ܕܘܬ 834	ܡܚܟܓܐܠ 238	ܡܩܩܡ 265
ܕܘܘܘܒܟܠܐ 672	ܡܝ 501	ܡܩܩܡܐܠ 401
ܕܘܢܝ 323	ܡܝܓܣܡܢܠܐ 749	ܡܢܠܐ 715
ܕܘܐܠ 885	ܡܝܟܡ 625	ܡܢܠܐ 387
ܕܘܣܓܐܠ 372	ܡܝܪܐ 373	ܡܣ 651
ܕܘܣܢܠܐ 40	ܡܝܙ 82	ܡܥܝܟܠܐ 232
ܕܘܣܣܢܠܐ 673	ܡܥܐܠ 201	ܡܥܠ 428
ܕܦ 274	ܡܘܓܗܘܙܠܐ 502	ܡܥܟܓܠܐ 131

164 ܡܶܩܛܰܢܐ	548 ܐܳܬܳܐ	477 ܐܰܬܗܘ
416 ܡܶܩܰܕ	626 ܐܳܬܶܒ	95 ܐܰܬܰܝ
716 ܡܶܩܠܐ	676 ܐܳܬܘܕܘܬܐ	795 ܐܰܬܝܼܢܐ
119 ܡܶܩܠܳܐ	374 ܐܳܬܒ	719 ܐܳܬܝܼܬܐ
388 ܡܶܩ	101 ܐܳܬܘܒ	720 ܐܰܬܺܢܝ
76 ܡܶܕܐܳܐ	627 ܐܳܬܘܪܝܰܐ	796 ܐܰܬܺܢܐ
228 ܡܶܕܕܓܐ	889 ܐܳܬܘܟܢܐ	890 ܐܰܬܡܠ
652 ܡܶܕܝܼܐ	677 ܐܳܬܘܚܝܐ	528 ܐܰܬܺܢ
257 ܡܶܕܢܐ	717 ܐܳܬܘܥܚܝܐ	97 ܐܰܬܢܝ
380 ܡܶܕܢܐܬܶܐ	718 ܐܳܬܘܪܐ	751 ܐܰܬܢܺܝܟܠܐ
357 ܡܶܕܢܚܐ	678 ܐܳܫܘܢܚܐ	891 ܐܰܬܢܶܒ
189 ܡܶܕܢܳܐܐ	230 ܐܳܫܡܝܰܗ	220 ܐܳܬܪܐ
476 ܡܶܕܢܐ	512 ܐܳܬܕܘܐܐ	721 ܐܳܬܪܘܚܝܐ
213 ܡܰܕܺܣܝܰܐ	513 ܐܰܬܐ	226 ܐܳܬܪܢܚ
527 ܡܝܐܐܪܓܐ	68 ܐܳܬܚܨܝܼܪܐ	179 ܐܳܬܬܕܘܫܚܐ
503 ܡܰܝܕܘܡ	142 ܐܳܬܟܳܠܐ	297 ܐܳܬܬܨܡܚܐ
463 ܐܳܬܰܙܬܐ	837 ܐܳܬܟܰܕܡ	679 ܐܳܬܰܡܕ

Section 9:
Skeleton Syriac Grammar

SKELETON SYRIAC GRAMMAR

By Sebastian P. Brock
Oriental Institute, University of Oxford

The following skeleton grammar is intended solely for reference. It abstracts the main features of Syriac morphology in tabular form.

Transcription Notes.

1. Vowels accompanied by *matres lectionis* (i.e. Ālaph, Waw, and Yôdh) are marked with circumflex (i.e. the sign ˆ); thus,

$\hat{e} = e + $ ālaph; $ = e + $ yodh;
$\hat{o} = o + $ waw;
$\hat{\imath} = i + $ yôdh;
$\hat{a} = a + $ ālaph.

2. Letters between parenthesis are not pronounced, but appear in the written form.
3. The transcriptions throughout this section follow East Syriac pronunciation, which is older than West Syriac pronunciation; thus,

E. Syr. $\bar{a}$ = W. Syr. $\bar{o}$;
E. Syr. *-hôn*, *-kôn*, and *-tôn* = W. Syr. *-hûn*, *-kûn*, and *-tûn*, respectively.

1. Nominal Endings.

The following table provides nominal endings. Notice that the emph. s. m. ending is the same as the abs. s. f. ending.

Num.	Gend.	State	Suffix		Num.	Gend.	State	Suffix	
sing.	masc.	absolute	nil		pl.	masc.	absolute	-*în*	
		construct	nil				construct	-*ay*	
		emphatic	-*â*				emphatic	-*ê*	
	fem.	absolute	-*â*			fem.	absolute	-*ān*	
		construct	-*at*				construct	-*āt*	
		emphatic	-*tâ*				emphatic	-*ātâ*	

2. Verbal System.

The most frequent verbal forms (also called *conjugations* in some grammatical literature) are three pairs (i.e. a total of six forms); each pair consists of two forms, the first being active and the second passive. The following table gives the three active forms, followed by their passive counterparts. In the table, 1, 2 and 3 indicate the first, second and third radicals, respectively.

Voice	No.	General meaning	Form	Pattern	Example
active	I	base form	p^{c}al	12a3 or 12e3	
	II	intensive	pa^{cc}el	1a22e3	
	III	extensive, causative	af^{c}el	'a12e3	
passive	I	base form	'etp^{c}el	'et12e3	
	II	intensive	'etpa^{cc}al	'et1a22a3	
	III	extensive, causative	'ettaf^{c}al	'etta12a3	

3. Verbal Inflexional Markers.

Each of the forms cited in section 2 above occurs in all of the following: perfect (denoting past tense), imperfect (denoting future), imperative, participles (active and passive; denoting present tense), and infinitive. In order to indicate the number, person and gender of a verb, Syriac uses *verbal inflexional markers*. These may take the form of prefixes, suffixes or both. The following table provides all the verbal inflexional markers. A slash, /, indicates an alternative form. Examples can be found in the verbal paradigms on p. 57 ff.

		Perfect Suff.		Imperfect Pref.	Suff.	
s.	3 m.	nil		ne-	nil	
	f.	-at		te-	nil	
	2 m.	-t		te-	nil	
	f.	-t(y)		te-	-în	
	1 c.	-et		'e-	nil	
p.	3 m.	-(w)		ne-	-ôn[1]	
	f.	nil/-(y)*		ne-	-ān*	
	2 m.	-tôn[2]		te-	-ôn[3]	
	f.	-tên*		te-	-ān*	
	1 c.	-n/-nan		ne-	nil	

(Cont.)

		Imperative Suff.		Participles Suff.	
s.	3 m.			nil	
	f.			-â	
	2 m.			nil	
	f.	-(y)			
	1 c.				
p.	3 m.			-în[4]	
	f.			-ān*	
	2 m.	-(w)/-ûn			
	f.	-ên/-(y)*			
	1 c.				

Notes. * With *Seyame*, specially in W. Syr.

The above table is valid for all verbs in the six forms listed under section 2 above, except that the imperfect preformative is n-/t- in the pa^{cc}el, and na-/ta-/'a- in the af^{c}el. The infinitive and the participle, however, differ from one form to another. The affixes of these are given in the following table.

---

[1] W. Syr. = -ûn «ܘܢ».
[2] W. Syr. = -tûn «ܬܘܢ».
[3] W. Syr. = -ûn «ܘܢ».
[4] = -ên «ܝܢ» with verbs whose third radical is Ālaph.

Voice	Form	Infinitive Pref.	Suff.			Participle Pref.	
active	I	*me-*	nil		ܡ	nil	
	II	*m-*	*-û*	ܘ	ܡ	*m-*	ܡ
	III	*ma-*	*-û*	ܘ	ܡ	*ma-*	ܡ
passive	I	*met-*	*-û*	ܘ	ܡܬ	*met-*	ܡܬ
	II	*met-*	*-û*	ܘ	ܡܬ	*met-*	ܡܬ
	III	*metta-*	*-û*	ܘ	ܡܬܬ	*metta-*	ܡܬܬ

4. Verbal Paradigms.

The following table gives the verbal patterns of some of the main forms. For examples of all the categories listed in the table, refer to the verbal paradigms on p. 57 ff. In the table, 1, 2 and 3 indicate the first, second and third radicals, respectively. The patterns are given for the s. 3 m. verb.

Note. Initial *Nun* verbs follow the pattern of the regular or strong verbs, except that, when ever there is a sequence in the form -a/e12-, the first radical as assimilated into the second (i.e. -a/e22-).

Form			Strong	1st rad. *Yôdh*	3rd rad. *Ālaph*	2nd rad. *Waw/Yôdh*	Double *2 = 3*
			ܩܛܠ	ܝܬܒ	ܒܟܐ	ܩܘܡ، ܣܝܡ	ܒܙܙ
I	act.	perf.	12a3	î2e3	12â	lā3	la2
			ܩܛܠ	ܝܬܒ	ܒܟܐ	ܩܡ، ܣܡ	ܒܙ
		impf.	ne12ô3	nî2a3	ne12ê	nlû3 / nlî3	ne11ô2
			ܢܩܛܘܠ	ܢܐܬܒ	ܢܒܟܐ	ܢܩܘܡ، ܢܣܝܡ	ܢܒܘܙ
		part.	lā2e3	= strong	lā2ê	lā'e3	lā'e3
			ܩܛܠ	ܝܬܒ	ܒܟܐ	ܩܐܡ[5]	ܒܐܙ[6]
		infin.	me12a3	mî2a3	me12â	mlā3	me11a3
			ܡܩܛܠ	ܡܐܬܒ	ܡܒܟܐ	ܡܩܡ	ܡܒܙ
II	act.	perf.	la22e3	= strong	la22î	= strong	= strong
			ܩܛܠ	ܝܬܒ	ܒܟܝ	ܩܝܡ	ܒܙܙ
		impf.	nla22e3	= strong	nla22ê	= strong	= strong
			ܢܩܛܠ	ܢܝܬܒ	ܢܒܟܐ	ܢܩܝܡ	ܢܒܙܙ
		part.	mla22e3	= strong	mla22ê	= strong	= strong
			ܡܩܛܠ	ܡܝܬܒ	ܡܒܟܐ	ܡܩܝܡ	ܡܒܙܙ
		infin.	mla22ā3û	= strong	mla22āyû	= strong	= strong
			ܡܩܛܠܘ	ܡܝܬܒܘ	ܡܒܟܝܘ	ܡܩܝܡܘ	ܡܒܙܙܘ

5 The /'/ is pronounced as /y/ in W. Syr., hence /qoyem/.
6 W. Syr. pronunciation /boyez/.

III	act.	perf.	'a12e3	'aw/y2e3	'a12î	'alî3	'alle2
			ܐܰܩܛܶܠ	ܐܰܘܬܶܒ	ܐܰܒܥܺܝ	ܐܰܩܺܝܡ	ܐܰܒܶܙ
		impf.	na12e3	naw/y2e3	na12ê	nlî3	nalle2
			ܢܰܩܛܶܠ	ܢܰܘܬܶܒ	ܢܰܒܥܶܐ	ܢܩܺܝܡ	ܢܰܒܶܙ
		part.	ma12e3	maw/y2e3	ma12ê	mlî3	malle3
			ܡܰܩܛܶܠ	ܡܰܘܬܶܒ	ܡܰܒܥܶܐ	ܡܩܺܝܡ	ܡܰܒܶܙ
		infin.	ma12ā3û	maw/y2ā3û	ma12āyû	mlā3û	mallā3û
			ܡܰܩܛܳܠܽܘ	ܡܰܘܬܳܒܽܘ	ܡܰܒܥܳܝܽܘ	ܡܩܳܡܽܘ	ܡܰܒܳܙܽܘ
I	pass.	perf.	'et12e3	'etî2e3	'et12î	= III pass.	= strong
			ܐܶܬܩܛܶܠ	ܐܶܬܺܝܬܶܒ	ܐܶܬܒܥܺܝ	ܐܶܬܬܩܺܝܡ	ܐܶܬܒܙܶܙ
		impf.	net12e3	netî2e3	net12ê	= III pass.	= strong
			ܢܶܬܩܛܶܠ	ܢܶܬܺܝܬܶܒ	ܢܶܬܒܥܶܐ	ܢܶܬܬܩܺܝܡ	ܢܶܬܒܙܶܙ
		part.	12î3	î2î3	12ê	1î3	= strong
			ܩܛܺܝܠ	ܝܺܬܺܝܒ	ܒܥܶܐ	ܩܺܝܡ	ܒܙܺܝܙ
			met12e3	metî2e3	met12ê	= III pass.	= strong
			ܡܶܬܩܛܶܠ	ܡܶܬܺܝܬܶܒ	ܡܶܬܒܥܶܐ	ܡܩܳܡ	ܡܶܬܒܙܶܙ
		infin.	met12ā3û	metî2ā3u	met12āyû	= III pass	= strong
			ܡܶܬܩܛܳܠܽܘ	ܡܶܬܺܝܬܳܒܽܘ	ܡܶܬܒܥܳܝܽܘ	ܡܶܬܬܩܳܡܽܘ	ܡܶܬܒܙܳܙܽܘ
II	pass.	perf.	'etla22a3	= strong	'etla22î	= strong	= strong
			ܐܶܬܩܰܛܰܠ	ܐܶܬܝܰܬܰܒ	ܐܶܬܒܰܥܺܝ	ܐܶܬܩܰܝܰܡ	ܐܶܬܒܰܙܰܙ
		impf.	netla22a3	= strong	netla22ê	= strong	= strong
			ܢܶܬܩܰܛܰܠ	ܢܶܬܝܰܬܰܒ	ܢܶܬܒܰܥܶܐ	ܢܶܬܩܰܝܰܡ	ܢܶܬܒܰܙܰܙ
		part.	mla22a3	= strong	mla22ay	= strong	= strong
			ܡܩܰܛܰܠ	ܡܝܰܬܰܒ	ܡܒܰܥܰܝ	ܡܩܰܝܰܡ	ܡܒܰܙܰܙ
			metla22a3	= strong	metla22ê	= strong	= strong
			ܡܶܬܩܰܛܰܠ	ܡܶܬܝܰܬܰܒ	ܡܶܬܒܰܥܶܐ	ܡܶܬܩܰܝܰܡ	ܡܶܬܒܰܙܰܙ
		infin.	metla22ā3û	= strong	metla22āyû	= strong	= strong
			ܡܶܬܩܰܛܳܠܽܘ	ܡܶܬܝܰܬܳܒܽܘ	ܡܶܬܒܰܥܳܝܽܘ	ܡܶܬܩܰܝܳܡܽܘ	ܡܶܬܒܰܙܳܙܽܘ

		III pass. perf.	'etta12a3	'ettaw2a3	'etta12î	'ettlî3	'ettalla2
		impf.	netta12a3	nettaw2a3	netta12ê	nettlî3	nettalla2
		part.	ma12a3	maw/y2a3	ma12ay	mlā3	malla3
			metta12a3	mettaw/y2a3	metta12ê	mettlî3	mettalla3
		infin.	metta12ā3û	mettaw/y2ā3û	metta12āyû	mettlā3û	mettallā3û

5. Suffixes: Main Characteristics.

The following suffixes attach to verbs and nouns. In the following table a slash, /, indicates variants.

		Suffix		Notes
s.	3 m.	-h / -why / -yhy		
	f.	-h		always with a supralinear point
	2 m.	-k		
	f.	-ky		
	1 c.	-y		with verbs: -ny
p.	3 m.	-hwn		
	f.	-hyn		
	2 m.	-kwn		
	f.	-kyn		
	1 c.	-n		

6. Suffixes to Nouns.

The following suffixes attach to nouns.

		to sing. & fem. pl. nouns		to masc. pl. nouns	
s.	3 m.	-eh		-aw(h)y	
	f.	-āh		-êh	
	2 m.	-āk		-ayk	
	f.	-ek(y)		-ayk(y)	
	1 c.	-(y)		-ay	
p.	3 m.	-hôn		-ayhôn	
	f.	-hên		-ayhên	
	2 m.	-kôn		-aykôn	
	f.	-kên		-aykên	
	1 c.	-an		-ayn	

7. Suffixes to Verbs.

The following three tables provide the object suffixes which attach to the perfect, imperfect and imperative of verbs.

i. Suffixes attached to perfect verbs.

Suffix		To Verbs s. 3 m. & f., s. 1 c.	To Verbs s. 2 m., all other pl. except pl. 3 m.	To Verbs s. 2 f.	To Verbs pl. 3 m.
s.	3 m.	-eh	-āy(h)y	-îw(h)y	-(h)y
	f.	-āh	-āh	-îh	-h
	2 m.	-āk	-āk		-k
	f.	-ek(y)	-ek(y)		-k(y)
	1 c.	-an(y)	-ān(y)	-în(y)	-n(y)
p.	3 m.				
	f.				
	2 m.	-kôn	-kôn		-kôn
	f.	-kên	-kên		-kên
	1 c.	-an	-ān	-în	-n

ii. Suffixes attached to imperfect verbs.

Suffix		To Verbs s. 3 m. & f., s. 2 m. s. & p.1 c.	To Verbs s. 2 f., all other pl.
s.	3 m.	-îw(h)y/-eh	-āy(h)y / -eh
	f.	-îh	-āh
	2 m.	-āk	-āk
	f.	-ek(y)	-ek(y)
	1 c.	-an(y)	-ān(y)
p.	3 m.		
	f.		
	2 m.	-kôn	-ākôn
	f.	-kên	-ākên
	1 c.	-an	-ān

iii. Suffixes attached to imperative verbs.

Suffix		To Verbs s. 2 m.	To Verbs s. 2 f.	To Verbs p. 2. m. & f.
s.	3 m.	-āy(h)y	-îw(h)y	-āy(h)y
	f.	-êh	-îh	-āh
	1 c.	-ayn(y)	-în(y)	-ān(y)
p.	1 c.	-ayn	-în	-ān

Notice that in the p^cal perfect, the patterns of verbs change with suffixes according to the following table:

	Verb	Patterns without Suffix	With suffixes: except pl. 2	With suffixes: only pl. 2
s.	3 m.	12a3 ܡܲܓܸܠ	1a23- ܡܲܓܸܠ	12a3 ܡܲܓܸܠ
	f.	1e23at ܡܸܓܠܲܬ	12a3t- ܡܲܓܸܠܬ-	1e23at ܡܸܓܠܲܬ-
	2 m.	12a3t ܡܲܓܸܠܬ	12a3t- ܡܲܓܸܠܬ-	
	f.	12a3t(y) ܡܲܓܸܠܬܝ	12a3t- ܡܲܓܸܠܬ-	
	1 c.	1e23et ܡܸܓܠܸܬ	12a3t- ܡܲܓܸܠܬ-	12a3t- ܡܲܓܸܠܬ-
p.	3 m.	12a3(w) ܡܲܓܸܠܘ	1a23û- ܡܲܓܸܠܘ-	1a23û ܡܲܓܸܠܘ-
	f.	12a3 / 12a3(y) ܡܲܓܸܠ	1a23- ܡܲܓܸܠ	12a3- ܡܲܓܸܠ
	2 m.	12a3tôn ܡܲܓܸܠܬܘܢ	12a3tôn- ܡܲܓܸܠܬܘܢ-	
	f.	12a3tên ܡܲܓܸܠܬܝܢ	12a3tên- ܡܲܓܸܠܬܝܢ-	
	1 c.	12a3n ܡܲܓܸܠܢ	12a3n- ܡܲܓܸܠܢ-	12a3n- ܡܲܓܸܠܢ-

8. Index of Prefixes and Suffixes.

i. Prefixes.

Prefix		Denotes	
'-	ܐܲ	1. 'e-	impf. p^{c}al and pa^{cc}el s. 1 c.
	ܐܲ	2. 'a-	a. perf. af^{c}el s. 3 m.
			b. impf. af^{c}el s. 1 c.
'et-	ܐܸܬ	1.	all passives, perf. and impt.
		2.	all passives, impf. s. 1 c.
d-	ܕ	1.	relative particle.
		2.	genitive particle.
		3.	introducing subordinate clause.
l-	ܠ	1.	preposition *to, for*.
		2.	introducing defined direct object.
m-	ܡ	1.	all active infinitives.
		2.	pa^{cc}el and af^{c}el participles.
		3.	some nouns (usually of place).

met-	ܡܬ݂	1.	all passive infinitives and participles.
n-	ܢ	1.	impf. s. 3 m.; pl. 3 m. & f.; pl. 1 c.
net-	ܢܬ݂	1.	impf. passive s. 3 m.; pl. 3 m. & f.; pl. 1 c.
t-	ܬ݂	1.	impf. s. 3 f.; s. 2 m. & f.; pl. 2 m. & f.
		2.	some nouns.
tet-	ܬܬ݂	1.	impf. passive s. 3 f.; s. 2 m. & f.; pl. 2 m. & f.

ii. Suffixes (an asterisk, *, denotes forms where there will also be a prefix).

Suffix			Denotes
-'	ܐ	1. -â	nominal ending for: a. emph. s. m. b. abs. s. f.
	ܐ̈	2.	nominal ending for emph. pl. m. (with *Seyame* ¨).
-'yt	ܐܝܬ݂	1.	adverbial suffix.
-h	ܗ	1. -eh	s. 3 m. suffix to: a. nouns: s. m. & f.; pl. f. b. verbs: perf. s. 3 m. & f.; s. 1 c.; impf.* (rare).
	ܗ̇	2. -āh	s. 3 f. suffix to: a. nouns. b. verbs: perf. and impf.*.
	ܘܗ̇	3. -ūh	s. 3 f. suffix to verbs perf. pl. 3 m.
-hwn	ܗܘܢ	1. -hôn	pl. 3 m. suffix to nouns.
-hy	ܗܝ	1. -ū(h)y	s. 3 m. suffix to verbs perf. pl. 3 m.
-hyn	ܗܝܢ	1. -hên	pl. 3 f. suffix to nouns.
-w	ܘ	1.	verbal ending perf. pl. 3 m.
		2.	with prefix *m-* or *mt-*, infinitive* pa^{cc}el and af^{c}el.
-why	ܘܗܝ	1. -aw(h)y	s. 3 m. suffix to pl. m. nouns.
-wt-	ܘܬ݂	1. -ūt-	abstract noun ending with suffixes.
		2. -ūt-	with prefix *m-* or *mt-*, infinitive* ending of pa^{cc}el and af^{c}el with suffixes.
-y	ܝ	1. -(y)	s. 1 suffix to s. nouns.
	ܝ̈	2. -ay	s. 1 suffix to pl. nouns.
		3. -ay	construct, pl. m. nouns.
		4. -ay	verbal ending for third radical Ālaph verbs perf. pl. 3 f.
		5. -y	verbal ending for perf. pl. 3 f. (all other verbs; late, W. Syr. orthography).
-y'	ܝܐ	1. -ayyâ	emphatic pl. m. nouns with 3rd radical Ālaph (with *Seyame*).
		2. -āyâ	adjectival suffix; pl. āyê (with *Seyame*).
-yh	ܝܗ	1. îh	s. 3 f. suffix to verbs: a. perf. s. 2 f. b. impf.* s. 3 m.; s. 2 m.; s. & pl. 1 c. c. impt. s. 2 f.
		2. -êh	s. 3 f. suffix to:

			a. nouns: pl. m.
			b. verbs: impt. s. 2 m.
-yhwn	ܝܗܘܢ	1. -ayhôn	pl. 3 m. suffix to nouns pl. m.
-yhy	ܝܗܝ	1. -āy(h)y	s. 3 m. suffix to verbs:
			a. perf. pl. 3 f.; s. 2 m.; pl. 2 m. & f.; pl. 1 c.; and s. 3 m. of 3rd rad. Ālaph verbs.
			b. impf.* s. 2 f.; pl. 3 m. & f.; pl. 2 m. & f.
			c. impt. s. 2 m.; pl. 2 m.
-yhyn	ܝܗܝܢ	1. -ayhên	pl. 3 f. suffix to nouns pl. m.
-ywhy	ܝܘܗܝ	1. -îw(h)y	s. 3 m. suffix to verbs:
			a. perf. s. 2 f.
			b. impf.* s. 3 m.; s. 2 m.; pl. 1 s.
			c. impt. s. 2 f.
-yk	ܝܟ	1. -ayk	s. 2 m. suffix to nouns pl. m.
-yky	ܝܟܝ	1. -ayk(y)	s. 2 f. suffix to nouns pl. m.
-ykwn	ܝܟܘܢ	1. -aykôn	pl. 2 m. suffix to nouns pl. m.
-ykyn	ܝܟܝܢ	1. -aykên	pl. 2 f. suffix to nouns pl. m.
-yn	ܝܢ	1. -în	a. nominal ending of abs. pl. m.
			b. part. endings of pl. m.
			c. impf. ending for s. 2 f.
			d. pl. 1 suffix to verbs: perf. s. 2 f.; impt. s. 2 f.
		2. -ên	a. part. pl. m. verbs 3rd rad. Ālaph.
			b. impt. pl. 2 f.
		3. -ayn	pl. 1 suffix to:
			a. nouns pl. m.
			b. verbs impt. s. 2 m.
-yny	ܝܢܝ	1. -ayn(y)	s. 1 suffix to impt. s. 2 m.
		2. -în(y)	s. 1 suffix to impt. s. 2 f.
-ynn	ܝܢܢ	1. -înan	part. pl. m. + pl. 1 c. pronoun.
		2. -ênan	part. pl. m. verbs 3rd rad. Ālaph + pl. 1 c. pronoun.
-ytwn	ܝܬܘܢ	1. -îtôn	part. pl. m. + pl. 2 m. pronoun.
		2. -êtôn	part. pl. m. verbs 3rd rad. Ālaph + pl. 2 m. pronoun.
-k	ܟ	1. -āk	s. 2 m. suffix to:
			a. nouns: s. m. & f.; pl. f.
			b. verbs perf. (see section 7 above).
			c. verbs impf.*
		2. -ûk	s. 2 m. suffix to verbs perf. pl. 3 m.
-kwn	ܟܘܢ	1. -kôn	pl. 2 m. suffix to:
			a. nouns s. m. & f.; pl. f.
			b. verbs perf. (all persons).
			c. verbs impf.* s. 3 m. & f.; s. & pl. 1.
		2. -ākôn	pl. 2 m. suffix to verbs impf.* pl. 3 m. & f.
-ky	ܟܝ	1. -ek(y)	s. 2 f. suffix to:
			a. nouns s. m. & f.; pl. f.
			b. verbs perf. and impf.*
		2. -ûk(y)	s. 2 f. suffix to verbs perf. pl. 3 m.
-kyn	ܟܝܢ	1. -kên	pl. 2 f. suffix to:
			a. nouns s. m. & f.; pl. f.

			b. verbs perf.
			c. verbs impf.* s. 3 m. & f.; s. & pl. 1.
		2. -ākên	pl. 2 f. suffix to verbs impf.* pl. 3 m. & f.
-n	ܢ	1. -n	verbal ending perf. pl. 1.
		2. -an	pl. 1 suffix to:
			a. nouns: s. m. & f.; and pl. f.
			b. verbs perf. s. 3 m. & f.
			c. verbs impf.* s. 3 m. & f.; s. 2 m.
		3. -ān	
			a. nominal ending for abs. pl. f.
			b. verbal ending for impf.* pl. 3 f.; pl. 2 f.
			c. pl. 1 suffix to verbs perf. s. 2 m.; pl. 3 f.; pl. 2 m. & f.
			d. pl. 1 suffix to verbs impf.* s. 2 f.; pl. 3 m. & f.; pl. 2 m. & f.
			e. pl. 1 suffix to verbs impt. pl. 2 m.
			f. part. s. f. + s. 1 c. pronoun.
		4. -ên	part. s. m. verbs 3rd rad. Ālaph + s. 1 c. pronoun (rare).
		5. -ûn	pl. 1 suffix to verbs perf. pl. 3 m.
-n'	ܢܐ	1. -nā	part. s. m. + s. 1 c. pronoun.
		2. -ānā	part. s. f. + s. 1 c. pronoun.
		3. -ênā	part. s. m. verbs 3rd rad. Ālaph + s. 1 c. pronoun.
-nn	ܢܢ	1. -ānan	part. pl. f. + pl. 1 c. pronoun.
-ny	ܢܝ	1. -an(y)	s. 1 suffix to verbs:
			a. perf. s. 3 m. & f.
			b. impf.* s. 3 m. & f.; s. 2 m.
		2. -ān(y)	s. 1 suffix to verbs:
			a. perf. s. 2 m.; pl. 3 f.; pl. 2 m. & f.
			b. impf.* s. 2 f.; pl. 3 m. & f.; pl. 2 m. & f.
			c. impt. pl. 2 m.
			d. part. s. f. + s. 1 c. pronoun.
		3. -ûn(y)	s. 1 suffix to verbs perf. pl. 3 m.
-t	ܬ	1. -at	ending for:
			a. nouns const. s. f.
			b. verbs perf. s. 3 f.
			c. part. s. m. + s. 2 m. pronoun.
		2. -āt	nominal ending for const. pl. f.
		3. -t	verbal ending for perf. s. 2 m.
		4. -et	verbal ending for s. 1. c.
		5. -êt	part. s. m. verbs 3rd rad. Ālaph + s. 2 m. pronoun.
-t'	ܬܐ	1. -tâ	nominal emph. s. f. ending.
	ܬܐ̈	2. -ātâ	nominal emph. pl. f. ending (with *Seyāme*).
-twn	ܬܘܢ	1. -tôn	verbal ending for perf. pl. 2 m.
-ty	ܬܝ	1. -t(y)	
			a. s. 1 suffix to f. nouns.
			b. verbal ending: perf. s. 2 f.
			c. part. s. f. + s. 2 f. pronoun.
-tyn	ܬܝܢ	1. -tên	verbal ending: perf. pl. 2 f.
		2. -ātên	part. pl. f. + pl. 2 f. pronoun.

9. Some Frequent Particles.

'aykannâ d-	+ impf.	ܐܰܝܟܰܢܳܐ ܕ	"so that"
dlâ	+ noun	ܕܠܳܐ	"without"
"	+ verb (perf.)	"	"who has/have not"
"	+ verb (impf.)	"	"lest"
kad	+ verb (perf.)	ܟܰܕ	"when"
"	+ participle	"	"while" (or English participle)
mâ d-	+ verb (perf.)	ܡܳܐ ܕ	"when"
meṭṭol d-	+ verb (perf.)	ܡܶܛܽܠ ܕ	"because"
"	+ verb (impf.)	"	"so that"

10. Syntax of kûll - ܟܽܠ.

kul + abs. = "each..., every ..."   e.g. *kul (')nāš*, "every one"
kull- + anticipatory suffix + emphatic = "all the ..."   e.g. *kulleh ʿālmâ*, "all the world"
kul + d- = "everyone who ...."   e.g. *kul d-qārê*, "everyone who calls"

Section 10: Bibliography

General Information.

The following bibliography is selective: it is aimed at providing a list of works which can be of use to the student of New Testament Syriac. Works out of print are indicated by 'op'; these are included only in cases when no later work is a substitute for them. New Testament versions other than the Peshitta are also included for the convenience of the student. Early editions are excluded.

Addresses.

Addresses of publishing houses holding works in print or reprinted works are also provided. Note that these addresses were produced at the time of publishing this book (1993).

New Testament Editions

The standard edition of the Syriac New Testament is that of the British and Foreign Bible Society (BFBS), now reprinted by the United Bible Society (UBS) in the 1988 and subsequent editions; prior editions of the UBS were based on Lee's edition. For a detailed account on the contents of this edition, see G. Kiraz's *Concordance to the Syriac New Testament*, p. xiv-xv.

- Old Syriac.
  - A. Lewis, *The Old Syriac Gospels or Evangelion Da-Mepharreshe*. (London: 1910; reprinted by Curt Daniel.)
    [Based on the Sinai palimpsest (S).]
  - F. C. Burkitt, *Evangelion Da-Mepharreshe: The Curetonian Version of the Four Gospels*, vol. 1. (Cambridge University Press: 1904; reprinted by Curt Daniel.)
    [Based on the Curetonian (C) MS.]

  The texts of S and C are reprinted in G. Kiraz's 'A Comparative Edition', see under 'Tools' below.

- Peshitta.
  - British and Foreign Bible Society, *The New Testament in Syriac*. (London: 1920 and reprints.)
    [This is the standard text of the Syriac New Testament (Peshitta) in vocalized Serto (Western) script. The Gospels are taken from Pusey and Gwilliam's *Tetraeuangelium Sanctum*; the Acts, James, 1 Peter, 1 John, the Pauline Epistles and Hebrews from an edition prepared by Gwilliam and J. Pinkerton; the Minor Catholic Epistles from Gwynn's *Remnants*; and the Apocalypse from Gwynn's *The Apocalypse*. See below for details.]
  - United Bible Society, *Syriac Bible*.
    [New Testament prior to the 1988 edition is from Lee's edition. The 1988 and subsequent editions are taken from the BFBS edition reorganized in two columns.]
  - American Bible Society, Syriac Bible. (Urmia: 1852.)
    [In two columns, the first Peshitta and the second in the Urmia vernacular, op.]
  - *Biblia Sacra juxta versionen simplicem Quae dicitur Pschitta*, vol. III. (Mosul: 1891.)
    [op.]
  - S. Lee, *Novum Testamentum Syriace*. (London: 1816.)
    [Reprinted by the UBS in editions prior to 1988.]
  - Pusey and Gwilliam, *Tetraeuangelium Sanctum*. (Oxford: The Clarendon Press, 1901.)
    [In vocalized Serto (Western) script with critical apparatus; text reprinted by BFBS. op.]
  - The Way International, *The Aramaic New Testament*. (New Knoxville: American Christian Press, 1983.)
    [In Estrangela script.]

- Philoxenian (As identified by Gwynn).
  - J. Gwynn, *Remnants of the Later Syriac Versions of the Bible*. (London: 1909; reprint by Academic Publishers Associated 1973.)
    [This work includes the Minor Catholic Epistles and John vii 53 - viii 12 (which are absent from the Peshitta).]
  - J. Gwynn, *The Apocalypse of St. John in a Syriac Version hitherto Unknown*. (Dublin, London: 1897; reprint by Academic Publishers Associated 1981.)
    [Includes an annotated reconstruction of the underlying Greek text.]

- Harklean.
  - J. White, *Sacrorum Evangeliorum Versio Syriaca Philoxeniana* (sic). (Oxford: The Clarendon Press, 1778.)
    [Harklean Gospels wrongly called 'Philoxenian' with Latin translation. op.]

- J. White, *Actuum Apostolorum et Epistolarum tam Catholicarum quam Paulinarum, Versio Syriaca Philoxeniana*. (Oxford: The Clarendon Press, 1803.)
  [Harklean Acts and Epistles wrongly called 'Philoxenian' with Latin translation. op.]
- G. Bernstein, *Das Heilige Evangelium des Iohannes*. (Leipzig: 1853.)
  [The Gospel of St John in vocalized Serto (Western) script. Better text than that of White. op.]

For a new text of the Harklean see Kiraz's 'A Comparative Edition' (Gospels), and B. Aland and A. Juckel's 'Das Neue Testament in Syrischer Überlieferung' (Epistles). See under 'Tools' for more detail.

- Christian Palestinian Aramaic (CPA).
  - A. Lewis and M. Gibson, *The Palestinian Syriac Lectionary of the Gospels*. (London: 1899.)
    [Note that CPA is called in earlier literature 'Palestinian Syriac'. It is a Western Aramaic dialect written in a script related to Syriac. op.]

Translations.

- English
  - F. C. Burkitt, *Evangelion Da-Mepharreshe*, vol. 1.
    [Translation of the Old Syriac. See above under 'New Testament Editions'.]
  - R. Errico, *The Message of Matthew*.
    [From the Peshitta. See below under 'Tools'.]
  - G. M. Lamsa, *The Holy Bible*. (Philadelphia: 1968).
    [A translation of the Peshitta Bible. Not a very accurate translation.]
  - J. Murdock, The New Testament Syriac Peshitto. (New York: 1851; reprinted Boston: 1892.)
    [Not a very good translation! op]
  - The Way International Research Team (ed.), *Aramaic-English Interlinear New Testament*.
    [See below under 'Tools'.]
- Latin
  - Pusey and Gwilliam, *Tetraeuangelium Sanctum*.
    [Translation of the Peshitta. See above under 'New Testament Editions'. op.]

Tools.

- B. Aland and A. Juckel, *Das Neue Testament in Syrischer Überlieferung*. In Arbeiten zur Neutestamentlichen Textforschung. (Berlin, New York: Walter de Gruyter, 1986- .)
  [Gives the texts from Peshitta and Harklean, including citations of the Church Fathers, aligned under each other. Recommended for comparing different versions. Vol. 1 (1986) Minor Catholic Epistles, vol. 2 (1991) Roman and 1 Corinthians, (*forthcoming*) other Epistles.]
- R. Errico, *The Message of Matthew: An Annotated Parallel Aramaic and English Gospel of Matthew*. (Irvine, Ca: Noohra Foundation, 1991.)
  [Text in East Syriac characters with English translation and commentary.]
- T. Falla, *A Key to the Peshitta Gospels*. In New Testament Tools and Studies. (Leiden: E. J. Brill, 1991- .)
  [A very detailed lexicon, including the Greek behind the Syriac and a full reference list for each entry.]
- G. Kiraz, *A Computer-Generated Concordance to the Syriac New Testament according to the British and Foreign Bible Society's Edition*. (Leiden: E. J. Brill, 1993.)
  [A complete concordance with citations in six volumes.]

- G. Kiraz, *Lexical Tools to the Syriac New Testament*. (Sheffield Academic Press, 1993.)
  [Frequency lists and verbal paradigms. *The present work*.]

- G. Kiraz, *A Comparative Edition of the Syriac Gospels: Sinaticus, Curetonianus, Peshitta, Harklean*. (Leiden: E. J. Brill, *forthcoming*.)
  [Gives the texts of the various versions aligned under each other.]

- G. Kiraz, *Electronic Synopsis of the Four Gospels*. (Los Angeles: Alaph Beth Computer Systems, 1990.)
  [Computer program running under DOS, based on K. Aland's *Synopsis of the Four Gospels*.]

- The Way International Research Team (ed.), *The Concordance to the Peshitta Version of the Aramaic New Testament*. (New Knoxville: American Christian Press, 1985.)
  [Gives a reference list, without citations, for each entry.]

- The Way International Research Team (ed.), *Aramaic-English Interlinear New Testament*. Vol. 1 Matthew-John (1988), Vol. 2 Acts-Philemon (1988), Vol. 3 Hebrews-Revelation (1989). (New Knoxville: American Christian Press, 1988-89.)
  [Gives a Syriac-English interlinear on the right page, and two columns of English translation on the left page (1st column is King James, 2nd column from the Syriac).]

Lexica.

- W. Jennings, *Lexicon to the Syriac New Testament*. (Oxford: The Clarendon Press, 1926; reprinted by the Way International 1979.)
  [Recommended for students. The Way International obtained permission from Oxford University Press to reprint this work for sale *only* in the U.S.A.]

- G. Kiraz, *Lexicon of New Testament Syriac*. (*forthcoming*.)

- J. Payne Smith, *A Compendious Syriac Dictionary* (Oxford: The Clarendon Press, 1903; reprinted 1985.)
  [The standard general Syriac-English Lexicon, founded upon the *Thesaurus Syriacus* by R. Payne Smith.]

- The Way International Research Team (ed.), *English Dictionary Supplement to the Concordance to the Peshitta Version of the Aramaic New Testament*. (New Knoxville: American Christian Press, 1985.)
  [English-Syriac Index to the Way's *Concordance*.]

Falla's 'Key' gives an English index, and Kiraz's 'Concordance' gives an English-Syriac index. See under 'Tools' for more detail.

Studies.

- M. Black, 'The Syriac Versional Tradition', in K. Aland (ed.) *Die Alten Übersetzungen des Neuen Testaments, Die Kirchenväterzitate und Lektionare*. In Arbeiten zur Neutestamentlichen Textforschung, vol. 5. (Berlin, New York: Walter de Gruyter, 1972.)
  [A detailed survey of the various versions.]

- S. P. Brock, *The Bible in the Syriac Tradition*. In SEERI Correspondence Course on Syrian Christian Heritage, No. 1. (Kottayam: SEERI, 1989.)
  [A good introduction.]

- S. P. Brock, 'Syriac Versions', in *The Anchor Dictionary of the Bible*, vol. 6 pp. 794-9. (New York: Doubleday, 1992.)

- S. P. Brock, 'The Resolution of the Philoxenian/Harklean Problem', in E. J. Epp & G. D. Fee (eds), *Essays in Honour of B. M. Metzger*. (Oxford: The Clarendon Press, 1981, pp. 325-43.)

- F. C. Burkitt, *Early Eastern Christianity*, Chapter 2: The Bible in Syriac. (Oxford: The Clarendon Press, 1904).
  [op.]
- B. Metzger, *The Early Versions of the New Testament: Their Origin, Transmission and Limitations*, Chapter I: The Syriac Versions. (Oxford: The Clarendon Press, 1977).
  [An excellent account of the various Syriac versions.]
- A. Vööbus, *Studies in the History of the Gospel Text in Syriac I-II*. In Corpus Scriptorum Christianorum Orientalium, vols. 128/496, subsidia 3/79. (Louvain: Peeters, 1951/1987).
- A. Vööbus, *Early Versions of the New Testament*. (Stockholm, 1954).

General Grammars.

- J. Healey, *First Studies in Syriac*. In University Semitic Study Aids 6. (University of Birmingham, 1980, 2nd ed. 1986.)
  [Now available from Sheffield Academic Press.]
- G. Kiraz, *The Syriac Primer: Reading, Writing, Vocabulary and Grammar with Exercises and Cassette Activities*. In JSOT 5. (Sheffield Academic Press, 1985.)
  [Originally written for students of the Syriac Churches, its grammar is very limited but is recommended for oral reading using its cassette tape.]
- T. Muraoka, *Classical Syriac for Hebraists*. (Wiesbaden: Otto Harrassowitz, 1987.)
  [Recommended specially for students with background in Hebrew.]
- T. Nöldeke, *Compendious Syriac Grammar*, translated by J. Crichton. (London: 1904.)
  [The most detailed grammar; students may find it difficult to read!]
- T. Robinson, *Paradigms and Exercises in Syriac Grammar*. (Oxford: The Clarendon Press, 4th ed. reprinted 1978.)
  [Revised by L. Brockington.]

Publishing Houses

UBS edition of the Syriac Bible can be found in most Bible bookstores.

- Academic Publishers Associated (APA)
  Postbus 122, NL-3600 AC Maarssen, The Netherlands
- E. J. Brill
  Plantijnstraat 2, P. O. Box 9000, 2300 PA Leiden, The Netherlands
- Curt Daniel
  1209 N Hasvell Ave #L, Dallas Texas 75204
- Noohra Foundation.
  Irvine, California, U.S.A. [Not a complete address; Irvine telephone directory is (714)555-1212.]
- Peeters.
  P. B. 41, Bondgenotenlaan 153, B-3000 Leuven, Belgium.
- SEERI: St. Ephrem Ecumenical Research Institute
  Baker Hill, Kottayam-686 001, Kerala, India.
- Sheffield Academic Press
  343 Fulwood Road, Sheffield S10 3BP, England.
- The Way International
  P. O. Box 328, New Knoxville, OH 45871, U.S.A.

GORGIAS REPRINT SERIES

1. J. B. Segal, *Edessa 'The Blessed City'* (2001, based on the 1970 edition).
2. J. Hamlyn Hill, *The Earliest Life of Christ: The Diatessaron of Tatian* (2001, based on the 1910 2nd abridged edition).
3. Joseph Knanishu, *About Persia and Its People* (2001, based on the 1899 edition).
4. Robert Curzon, *Ancient Monasteries of the East, Or The Monasteries of the Levant* (2001, based on the 1849 edition).
5. William Wright, *A Short History of Syriac Literature* (2001, based on the 1894 edition).
6. Frits Holm, *My Nestorian Adventure in China, A Popular Account of the Holm-Nestorian Expedition to Sian-Fu and Its Results* (2001, based on the 1924 edition).
7. Austen Henry Layard, *Nineveh and Its Remains: an account of a visit to the Chaldean Christians of Kurdistan, and the Yezidis, or devil-worshipers; and an inquiry into the manners and arts of the ancient Assyrians*, Vol. 1 (2001, based on the 1850 5th edition).
8. Austen Henry Layard, *Nineveh and Its Remains*, Vol. 2 (2001, based on the 1850 5th edition).
9. Margaret Gibson, *How the Codex Was Found, A Narrative of Two Visits to Sinai From Mrs. Lewis's Journals 1892-1893* (2001, based on the 1893 edition).
10. Richard Davey, *The Sultan and His Subjects* (2001, based on the 1907 edition).
11. Adrian Fortescue, *Eastern Churches Trilogy: The Orthodox Eastern Church* (2001, based on the 1929 edition).
12. Adrian Fortescue, *Eastern Churches Trilogy: The Lesser*

Eastern Churches (2001, based on the 1913 edition).

13. Adrian Fortescue, *Eastern Churches Trilogy: The Uniate Eastern Churches: the Byzantine Rite in Italy, Sicily, Syria and Egypt* (2001, based on the 1923 edition).
14. A. V. Williams Jackson, *From Constantinople to the Home of Omar Khayyam: Travels in Transcaucasia and Northern Persia for Historic and Literary Research* (2001, based on the 1911 edition).
15. Demetra Vaka, *The Unveiled Ladies of Stamboul* (2001, based on the 1923 edition).
16. Oswald H. Parry, *Six Months in a Syrian Monastery: Being the Record of a Visit to the Head Quarters of the Syrian Church in Mesopotamia with Some Account of the Yazidis or Devil Worshipers of Mosul and El Jilwah, Their Sacred Book* (2001, based on the 1895 edition).
17. B. T. A. Evetts, *The Churches and Monasteries of Egypt and Some Neighbouring Countries, Attribted to Abû Sâlih the Armenian* (2001, based on the 1895 edition).
18. James Murdock, *The New Testament, Or the Book of the Holy Gospel of Our Lord and Our God Jesus the Messiah, A Literal Translation from the Syriac Peshita Version* (2001, based on the 1851 edition).
19. Gertrude Lowthian Bell, *Amurath to Amurath: A Five Month Journey Along the Banks of the Euphrates* (2001, based on the 1924 second edition).
20. Smith, George. *Assyrian Discoveries: An Account of Explorations and Discoveries on the Site of Nineveh, During 1873 and 1874* (2002, based on the 1876 edition).
21. Dalley, *Stephanie. Mari and Karana, Two Old Babylonian Cities* (2002, first US paperback edition).
22. Grant, *Asahel. The Nestorians or the Lost Tribe* (2002, based on the 1841 edition).
23. O'Leary, De Lacy. *The Syriac Church and Fathers* (2002, based on the 1909 edition).
24. Burkitt, F. C. *Early Christianity Outside the Roman Empire* (2002, based on the 1909 edition).
25. Wigram, W. A. *The Assyrians and Their Neighbours*

(2002, based on the 1929 edition).
26. Kiraz, George. *Lexical Tools to the Syriac New Testament* (2002, first US edition).
27. Margoliouth, G. *Descriptive List of Syriac and Karshuni Manuscripts in the British Museum Acquired Since 1873* (2002, based on the 1899 edition).

Printed by BoD™ in Norderstedt, Germany